The clockwork image

Erratum. On page 73 the fifth line of the second paragraph is missing. The sentences should read:

Are we not saying that, on this assumption, man is, if not 'nothing but' a machine, at least 'nothing but' an animal? Again, of course, we must watch the phrase, 'nothing but'.

The clockwork image

A Christian perspective on science

Donald M. MacKay

Inter-Varsity Press

INTER-VARSITY PRESS

Inter-Varsity Fellowship,
39 Bedford Square, London WC1B 3EY

© INTER-VARSITY PRESS, LONDON

First edition August 1974
ISBN 0 85110 377 4

Printed in Great Britain by
Hunt Barnard Printing Ltd, Aylesbury, Bucks.

For Robert,
Eleanor,
Janet,
Margaret and
– in due course –
David.

Contents

Preface

Too many people today, both Christian and non-Christian, tend to think of Science (with a capital S) as a bogey that threatens all moral and religious interpretations of life and its purpose. Before modern science appeared on the scene, religion may have happily frisked in the barest clothing of factual support; but now, here comes the Inspector.

No-one would deny, and few would regret, that the scientific climate of our time has withered many superstitions deep-rooted in past generations. It is perhaps only natural that those who see little distinction between superstition and biblical religion should expect the Christian faith itself to suffer progressively greater damage as science advances. Even Christians themselves are open to the temptation to think of 'faith' as something to be hung on to in the teeth of potentially hostile scientific discoveries, rather than viewing it as something which positively nourishes the spirit of scientific exploration. It is never too easy to distinguish hard scientific data from the philosophical extrapolations from them which are put about in the name of Science.

This book is addressed both to Christians who want to take stock of the scientific enterprise in the light of their faith, and to non-Christians who may wonder what Christian commitment would mean for their intellectual integrity in an age of mechanistic science. Its central theme is the *wholeness* of the view of our universe presented by biblical Christian theism: the essential, non-accidental harmony between the Christian doctrine of the natural world on the one hand and the spirit and practice of natural science on the other. This is illustrated first by a study of the scientific approach in general; then in terms of specific topics such as creation, scientific law and miracle, and the nature of man; and finally by showing how the Christian gospel itself invites the test of daily experience in essentially the same spirit of openness to evidence that animates the enquiring scientist.

The book is based largely on talks given to students and others over the past twenty years. Some of these were BBC broadcasts which presupposed no religious commitment on the part of the listeners; others were given at conferences of Christians and took rather more for granted. Despite extensive rewriting, differences in style and balance remain and will I hope be forgiven.

My wife and many friends have greatly helped in the shaping of the original talks and their subsequent revision, and my secretary, Miss M. A. Steele, has patiently coped with many retypings. My greatest single debt is to Professor R. Hooykaas of the Department of History of Science in Utrecht, who first taught me to recognize the liberating implications of biblical faith (as distinct from rationalistic biblicism) for the freedom of science and for properly critical thinking.

For permission to use material previously published or broadcast I am grateful to the British Broadcasting Corporation, the Council for Religious Instruction in Schools, Inc. of New York, and the Inter-Varsity Press, London.

D. M. MacKay.

Keele, May 1973.

1. The abuse of mechanistic thinking

There never was a time when the average man, at least in western countries, had open to him a wider range of choice on which to exercise his freedom. He has a greater geographical range, a greater power to command luxuries, a greater power to communicate with whomever he will, than any man alive in previous generations. Yet there has never been, perhaps, a time when more fears have been expressed that our own scientific and technological progress may end by stifling and destroying that same human freedom. Why should this be so? Is it just reactionary fear on the part of those ignorant of science and envious of its prestige? This may account for some of the emotional steam; but it would be a dangerously superficial answer to the warnings being sounded increasingly by sensitive thinkers of all religious and anti-religious complexions. Something, surely, is at least in danger of going badly wrong with our scientific civilization. Some genuine symptoms of disease must be present for so much fuss to be created.

The disease that threatens, I think, can be labelled 'machine-mindedness'. It is not essentially a problem of the set-up of our society, but rather of the presuppositions, the habits of thought, the dominant image which our fellow men have of themselves in their society and in their environment. In our age, when people look for explanations, the tendency more and more is to conceive of any and every situation that we are trying to understand by analogy with a machine. I do not think that any of us is free of this. There is a great tendency for all disciplines to take natural science, which means nowadays mechanistic science, as a standard model of the explanatory method, and even sometimes to twist their particular subject matter into as nearly scientific a mould as possible in order thereby to give it the greater respectability and objectivity.

Let me say at once that my own research department at Keele is concerned with the mechanisms of the brain, and that our working hypothesis is that the brain is capable of being studied as a mechanistic system. In order to explain human behaviour, chains of cause and effect can legitimately be sought and found in terms of physics, or physiology, or at still higher levels in terms of information-engineering[1] or psychology. The last thing I want to suggest is that there is anything improper about a mechanistic approach as such. What I do want to emphasize, however, is that a mechanistic approach adopted for scientific purposes is being abused if it leads to what I am calling machine-mindedness. There is all the difference in the world between describing and analysing a particular system as a mechanism, and claiming that the 'real' explanation, the only worthwhile or objective explanation to be had of the situation, is the explanation you get in terms of machine analogies.

Machine-mindedness is characterized not so much by what it affirms as by what it denies. For example, we are 'only cogs in an economic machine,' so there is nothing we can do to stop the economy from thundering on. We are 'only cogs in a political machine,' so there is no real choice before us; it is all determined by the machine. In many national elections people complain that they have no real freedom of choice because 'the machine' has not thrown up a suitable candidate for their particular outlook. The implication all along is that the machine is in command and that we have no access to the controls.

Come to think of it, perhaps we are only a mass of cogs ourselves. Physiologists and psychologists in their different languages suggest that, if you look scientifically at man, you can analyse his behaviour in terms of the interlocking

[1] The science of control and communication, including computer theory and the theory of automata.

of mechanistic 'cogs' just as you can any other aspect of the world. The conclusion drawn is that 'It ain't my fault, judge, it's me glands' – as the pretty girl is reputed to have said on an awkward occasion. No-one is ever 'guilty' – just 'sick' now and again.

We shall be looking in more detail later at this 'machine-minded' complex of ideas. We can see immediately, however, that it is *deterministic* and *depersonalizing*, with implications which are *demoralizing*. Clearly it throws up great obstacles to belief in and respect for human freedom and to our defence of it for thoughtful people today, whether in a secular or a religious context. I hope in due course to indicate some lines on which a proper remedy may be sought; but as our next step, I want to clear the ground by elaborating a little on the nature of the disease under each of these heads, and considering briefly some inadequate answers which are sometimes given to these threats to human freedom and dignity.

Determinism

Determinism is a slippery word, which is used in at least two different ways. It has one perfectly innocent meaning as the name of a particular scientific doctrine – a presupposition of the method of science – namely, that all physical events have physical causes. This doctrine may be false; but even if it were true it would not of itself say anything either for or against human freedom or morality. Secondly, however, the term may be used to mean the philosophical belief that the future is inevitable, that we have no real choices, that our sense of freedom is an illusion and our responsibility a figment of the moralist's imagination. It is in this latter sense that it forms an ingredient of machine-mindedness. Indeed it often claims logical support (il-legitimately, as we shall see in chapter 8) from scientific determinism in the first sense. To minimize confusion we shall use 'moral determinism' to refer to the second, machine-minded, variety.

As a result of the common confusion between the two,

people have sometimes been tempted to consider any weakening of scientific determinism as a blow to its parasitic namesake; but the following example shows that arguments on this basis are far from conclusive.

The irrelevance of the uncertainty principle

For many centuries scientific determinism had its stronghold in physics, particularly in Newtonian mechanics. There one assumes that from the initial state of any system, given the formulae that describe the motion of its constituents, one can predict its course at any future time. In a sense, therefore, the whole of the past and the present and the future is implicit in any complete description of any one state, any instantaneous snapshot, of the system. Over the last fifty years or so, however, it is possible to say (and indeed many people have used this as an argument for freedom) that physics has virtually abandoned its deterministic model of the world. In a sense this is true. Physics, at the level of the atom, has had to reckon with a snag that no-one had suspected. Energy (the coinage of interaction between physical systems) has turned out not to be continuously divisible. In any given situation, there is a 'smallest coin' or 'quantum' of possible energy-exchange. Since we cannot observe an atom (or anything else) without exchanging some energy with it, the new 'quantum theory' insists that a system observed must be a system disturbed to a finite extent. This leads to a fundamental kind of unpredictability that is associated with the name of Heisenberg. His famous principle of uncertainty (1927) implies, for example, that if we try to establish the exact position and speed of two atomic particles which are going to collide, we will never be able to do it accurately enough to determine exactly how they will rebound. The more exactly we observe the position, the less exactly we can specify the speed, and conversely. So the most elementary process envisaged by the mechanistic theory of classical physics – the action of one particle on another – turns out not to be precisely calculable. The cog-wheels of the classical clockwork model of the universe seem to have loose teeth! This has, of course, made a tremendous difference to the theory and practice of atomic physics. Moreover, it does mean that, in our present thought-model of the physical universe as a whole, absolute causality, in the sense of the unwinding of everything predictably from the initial conditions, has gone.

I want to suggest, however, that this would be a very inadequate and misleading answer to a 'moral determinist' of the sort that we are considering; for despite Heisenberg's revolutionary principle, we all know that clocks keep quite good time, the sun continues to rise relatively predictably, and other things that we depend on like boiling kettles continue to be reliable. Anyone who tries to make the indeterminacy of the models of physics a basis for restoring the idea of freedom, and combating machine-mindedness, must admit that at the level of man-sized objects this unpredictability normally makes no practical difference. It makes no practical difference in the sense in which the snapping of one hair in a rope makes no practical difference to the strength of the rope. Moreover, although most physicists today speak of atomic events as 'indeterminate', there have been those, including the great Einstein himself, who refused to concede that they were anything more than unpredictable-by-us. For both reasons, then, it would be very unwise to try to combat machine-mindedness and restore the idea that there is freedom in the world by laying stress on the indeterminacy of physical models.

Vitalism

There is a second line of approach which has sometimes been taken to try to clear an area for human freedom in this mechanistic picture. This is to suggest that living matter may obey different laws from non-living matter; a view which was labelled 'vitalism' in the nineteenth century. Today those who hold it would not wish to be called vitalists, because the term came to stand for specific theories now discredited; but the general idea is not dead. It claims that when we come to analyse the matter of which living organisms are composed we can no longer rely on the predictions that we would make if we were approaching the system from a mechanistic standpoint.

I should be the first to admit (and will later be insisting) that there is a qualitative difference between the kind of thinking we need to use in order to understand all aspects of a living organism, and the kind of thinking we use in studying either billiard balls or atomic physics. But I submit that it would be a great mistake if we thought that the answer to machine-mindedness was to adopt some kind of new vitalism and insist that the mechanistic scientist approaching living organisms must come unstuck somewhere along the road. It is, of course, conceivable; and it would be very exciting for those in my line of work if this were the case. It is quite possible that in neurobiology we may discover something so radically out of line with anything that our present science could imagine or predict that we will have to start again from scratch. This would be great fun; but I think that building our belief in freedom on a speculative hope of that kind would be a poor defence in the eyes of those who are committed to machine-mindedness.

I shall postpone suggesting any possible answer to moral determinism that would be stronger than these two until we have had a chance to focus more clearly on the issue.[2]

Depersonalization

In the second place, machine-mindedness devalues the dignity, uniqueness and worth of the human person. People are thought of as things. This aspect of it, I think, reveals what is most sinister in machine-mindedness, because it is of the essence of the attitude that you *separate* yourself from the human situation that you are conceiving under the image of a machine. You withdraw, as it were, from imaginative communication; you see the situation through a one-way screen, visualizing it as an assemblage of objects, as a spectacle for you, rather than as a community of others like you to whom you have obligations, and with whom you

[2] See chapter 8.

could have warm and rich relationships in mutual trust and self-giving. I am not of course suggesting that people consciously adopt this attitude in its pure form. For most of us it is a barely-sensed influence in the climate of thought of our time reflected mainly, perhaps, in the tone of the newspaper commentators, novelists and playwrights who shape our image of the world. But it is no less insidious and all-pervasive for that. More and more we are in danger of becoming at heart a society of spectators.

We see many signs of this at all levels today. Friendships become increasingly shallow as people tend to think of others as *manipulanda*, as entities to be manipulated, whether by the techniques of 'winning friends and influencing people' or by still more impersonal and more obviously unfriendly methods of 'one-upmanship' and the like. Families are in danger of becoming only huddles of mutual self-interest. If it suits their self-interest the members may occasionally be together; but the idea that each in a sense has his being in and through the others is decaying to an alarming extent in the eyes of many who study the social situation in our more 'cultured' communities. We are in danger of losing the concept of the family. Two or three generations ago the family meant not only father, mother and children but probably grandparents, the old unmarried aunt, and a great circle of other people who came and went because they belonged. Today one is lucky if the notion of the family means as much as father, mother and children.

I do not pretend that machine-minded thinking is the only factor at work in all this. One might cite, for example, the widespread increase in education and in wealth over the past century or so which has brought so much more independence on the part of children. But the mechanistic image of man undoubtedly provides what is thought to be a scientific sanction for these depersonalizing trends. They are considered to be 'in line with the progress of science'; and the more traditional attitudes and categories are felt to be vaguely 'pre-scientific'.

This depersonalization goes deeply into the domain of criminology. Even our criminals are sometimes robbed of the dignity of being blamed for their actions. I want to put it in this way because I think that offences can be committed against basic human rights by giving improper weight to psychiatric and other considerations of how a person becomes the way he is. It is thought by some would-be reformers that it is always more humane to treat a criminal as a sick object rather than to blame him as a responsible person. Whether or not there is sickness in the sense of a defect in the machinery, these people conclude from the mere fact that he did an antisocial act that he must be sick.

As we shall see in chapter 8, I do not deny that some people are criminals because they are sick. Indeed I would insist that, as we understand more of the working of the brain, we have a responsibility to sharpen our criteria for deciding when criminals are not fully responsible for their actions by reason of brain disorders. This evidence is something to be used positively. But I am trying to emphasize the other side of the picture which is so often neglected. My point is that if you take a man who had a genuine choice and exercised it, and then insist that because his decision was antisocial he is 'diseased' and must be treated only as an object, then you are doing perhaps the most serious damage you can to that man's moral dignity.

The university world, despite its professional concern for careful reasoning, is far from immune from these depersonalizing influences. Every day thousands of students read thousands of words along these lines, with visible results in the sapping of initiative, commitment and even clear thinking itself.

A variety of inadequate moves have been made to salvage personal categories in the face of machine-mindedness. Some, for instance, would argue that the whole vocabulary of personality is still perfectly usable as long as we see it as a shorthand for the mechanical. There is nothing wrong in speaking about a man's 'guilt', they would say, as long as you mean by it some complex of mechanistic conditionals: for example, 'This man is in such a state that if punished or if treated in such and such a way his behaviour will become or may become more socially acceptable.' Or there is no harm in speaking about 'love', provided that it is a shorthand for a disposition to interact with a member of the same or the opposite sex in some specified manner. Note that I am far from suggesting that a mechanistic description of this sort is necessarily untrue. The trouble with the machine-minded is only that they assume that it is the whole or 'real' truth, and that all else is merely a shorthand for it. I hope to show later that it would be a great mistake for us to concede this point.[3] Logically it would be as inept as to agree that an SOS morse message is not really a call for help, but only a shorthand for the physical description of the morse code signals.

Then there are others who argue that the use of personal language, however outdated by the march of mechanistic science, is justified because it is essential to bringing about the best kinds of interaction between people. Human freedom, for instance, may not be a valid concept, but it is a 'useful fiction'. It is hard to see how people of integrity can be expected to be satisfied by arguments of this order. In chapter 7 I shall argue that depersonalization can be tackled only by exposing the fallacy of machine-mindedness at a deeper level.

Demoralization

The third consequence of machine-mindedness is demoralization. If our whole world is a determinate system, so the argument goes, then for practical purposes what is, is right. It could be said that for philosophical consistency such a determinist ought to reject the notion of right altogether. But not all determinists are philosophically consistent. There is a widespread notion that by looking at the way things are you should be able to discover the way things ought to be. This is an attempted answer to the cry for values which goes up on all sides in our day, a cry resulting from the insecurity of feeling that all the things we instinctively recognize as morally important are questioned

[3] See chapter 4.

by Science with a capital S – by which people mean the image of the machine.

There are tempting but inadequate answers also to this kind of reasoning. Once again one finds people suggesting that it is useful to continue to employ value words even if you cannot find any justification for them in the machine image. It is useful to call actions 'good' or 'bad' for example, because your social system shows undesirable features if you do not. In this and in other ways attempts are made to preserve a structure of moral talk within a framework which is essentially mechanistic. The crucial question, of course, which is totally bypassed, is *to what end* this moral talk should be regarded as useful. Where does one get one's criterion of the useful? On exploration this turns out to be yet another of those dead-end streets, which we need to label as such before we seek more appropriate ways of meeting the demoralizing tendency of machine-mindedness.

Again, the idea that *evolutionary science* can be a source of morals, rather than at most a description of the mechanism by which species showing moral behaviour have come into being, is widely canvassed among those who accept the mechanistic habit of mind, but who wish to make a place for values within their closed system. But study the occurrence of words like 'good' and 'useful' as the evolutionist brings them in. What you discover is that at least some basic value judgments are imported into the situation rather than derived from it. If you overlook this, and assume that the implicit value judgment is part of the *scientific* data, then it may look as if you can come up with a plausible 'scientific' definition of what is good – for example, 'what is good is what causes the greatest number of a particular species to survive'. Provided one accepts this as part of the scientific data, then I think it is possible to go quite a long way towards showing, let us say, the usefulness of self-sacrifice, of forbearance, of peacemaking, and so on. But the problem is that this kind of logic is circular. It assumes at the outset that survival (or whatever) is already defined as *good*. (Would it have been 'good', for example, if Nazism had survived?) Any attempt to save our generation from the demoralizing effect of machine-mindedness by calling on evolutionary science, by looking at the way things have developed in order to get criteria of good, is in the end bankrupt. Those in the next generation who ask why they should or should not do this or that will be quick to spot the logical fallacy of any such argument.

Where should we start?

If, as I have suggested, these various remedies for machine-mindedness are dangerously inadequate, where must we begin in our critique? I believe that we must start by looking again at the scientific approach, and particularly at the religious ingredients that contributed to its development, in order to sense the contrast between it and the scientistic machine-mindedness that claims to be based on it. Next, we must uncover the logic (or lack of logic) that is used to gain scientific prestige for the destructive tendencies we have been considering. We shall find at the root of it an all-pervasive logical mistake – the fallacy of 'reductionism' or 'nothing-buttery'. When this has once been recognized, the case for machine-mindedness collapses so completely that the weaker arguments against it which we have been criticizing can be dismissed as superfluous.

Lastly, and more positively, we must ask how people can best be helped to come to terms properly with mechanistic science. In particular, does biblical Christianity offer a positive way of receiving with thankfulness the mechanistic science of our day, while still retaining the values that Christians regard as crucial and eternal? Is there a unifying perspective towards which we can think our way and which we can offer to the next generation, so that they may be able to enjoy the accelerating tempo of developments in mechanistic science without fear of determinism, depersonalization, or demoralization? Finally, if we can establish without obscurantism the fact that man is truly free, then we must ask the question, 'Free for what?' What is the wider context in which freedom makes sense, and how can it be presented in a way that makes sense to people today?

2. The scientific habit of mind

Christians are not alone in deploring the evils of machine-mindedness. Many atheistic or agnostic humanists are equally concerned at the damage being done to human values in the name of science, all the more so because, for most of them until recently (and for some of them still), faith in God has come to be replaced by faith in Science – with a capital S. True, there are still plenty of first-rank scientists today who are convinced Christians, and see each new scientific discovery as a fresh revelation of God's wisdom and power. But for many others it makes no sense to talk in such terms, and for the 'scientific humanist' in particular it counts as rank heresy. Man, he believes, is the master of things; and it is Science which at last has given him this mastery, and has in the process driven out and dethroned God.

Never mind for the moment whether we agree with this verdict. What we must try to do first, before we start arguing, is to understand how it is that the scientific way of knowing has come to earn so much respect – from Christians and non-Christians alike – and to see how it has brought about this change of mood towards religion in some of our contemporaries.

Science, as we know it, was born at a time when all men of learning were religious men, and when learning consisted mainly of knowing the pronouncements of ancient authorities, either Christian or pagan. The way to certainty, on any topic, was to think your way back from it to accepted first principles, to find an authority for it. If you wanted to know about the motions of the planets, for example, you went back to the first principle, expounded by Aristotle, that the only perfect motion was circular. Planets inhabited the realm of perfection, *ergo*, they moved in circles. The way in which a combination of new discoveries, social upheavals and biblical theology combined to change this attitude makes a fascinating story, which has been lucidly retraced in a recent book by Professor R. Hooykaas.[1] The founding of the Royal Society in 1668 may be taken as marking the official establishment of a totally new attitude to the problem of gaining reliable knowledge.

Of course anyone who wants to generalize, even about a single group of men living in the same period of time, is asking for trouble. Looking back over the varied history – and the varied membership – of the Royal Society, for instance, in the three centuries since its foundation, it may seem even more hopeless to try to define a single attitude shared by all its members. Strictly, of course, it is hopeless. Our notions of what makes a scientist have so grown and changed with time that we may wonder whether some of the early scientific Fellows would have stood a chance of election today! Yet, with all the changes, there is in fact an impressively insistent family likeness between scientists of every century, and of every race and creed. However hard it may be to pin down, it is there alright; and both its persistence and its success show that it answers to something fundamental about the world we live in. The modern scientific approach, in other words, was not so much an *invention*, as a *discovery*, by those seventeenth-century pioneers. The fact that it 'worked' was cumulative evidence that they had stumbled on something new about the nature of the universe, something that other ages, and other outlooks, had missed.

Respect for the natural world

What is it, then, that scientists, then and now, have in common? What are the telltale features of the scientific habit of mind? Historically, perhaps the first was a new kind

[1] *Religion and the Rise of Modern Science* (Scottish Academic Press, 1972).

of respect for the natural world as a worthy object of study. Nowadays we might scarcely regard this as a distinguishing feature; but that only shows the extent to which the new ideas have been accepted. Whatever truth there may be behind all the talk about 'two cultures', the scientific and the humane, there can be little doubt that the average layman today has absorbed far more than he realizes of the scientific habit of mind. Three centuries ago, the notion that ordinary matter could repay the attention of men of learning seemed absurd to many people. Only a few bold spirits ventured to believe that, if God thought matter worth creating, then they might find it worth studying, and might expect to be rewarded by discovering order and harmony in the most commonplace objects and events around them. By contrast with Plato's disregard for the material world, and the scholastic preference for arguing in an armchair from first principles, these men shared the burning conviction that what God had written in the book of nature (as they put it) ought to be read. Like the Bible itself, it could not fail to reward the man who approached it in the right spirit.

Some of us today believe that, if the reasoning of these pioneers had been remembered by the church, the later misunderstandings between scientists and churchmen need never have arisen. But however much the religious background has been overlaid in course of time, the respect for the natural world which it fostered still remains a hallmark of the scientist, whatever his creed. However unusual may be the phenomena he meets, he automatically credits them with having some rational explanation. His first instinct is to take the situation mentally to bits and look for some mechanism; some pattern of causal connection between the parts of the situation, which could have given rise to the phenomena that puzzle him.

The appeal to experience

Closely related to this respect for the rationality of nature is another characteristic feature – the scientist's insistence on the test of *experience* rather than rationalistic arguments from authority. It is possible to find fields even today in which rationalistic modes of thought are retained— Marxist sociology, for example, or (until recently) Lysenkoist biology. But for most scientists in most fields the appeal to dogmatic authority is abhorrent. Instead of arguing, for example, from what Aristotle said about the heavenly bodies, we would say that the obvious way to find out whether a planet could have satellites was to *go and look*. The obvious way? It was far from obvious to quite intelligent, honest people four centuries ago, for in Aristotle's system the idea was ruled out on principle. So when Galileo claimed to have seen satellites of Jupiter through his new-fangled telescope, it sounded to them like claiming to have discovered circles with a circumference more than π times their diameter. They had learned at school that this was impossible. Why should they bother to test such a crazy idea? Let Galileo waste his own time on it.

We had better look at this example rather closely, because I think it shows that the scientific principle here – the principle of appeal to experience – is not as simple as it is often made out to be. It is not just a matter of refusing to take anything on trust until we have tested it: that attitude leads to madness. Galileo himself, who was not entirely free of rationalistic tendencies, certainly did not dream of rejecting the scholastic theories until he met sufficient evidence to throw doubt on them; and he, like all of us, had to build his whole life on beliefs the bulk of which he could never test. No, what marked Galileo's attitude as scientific was not a craven fear of taking anything on trust, but an eagerness to do full justice to new facts of experience, whatever the cost to the theories he had held hitherto. He was eager, too, to put himself in the way of more facts, to turn the next page of the book of nature, hoping to have more of his ideas checked, or amplified, or corrected.

It is difficult for us now to imagine the sense of liberation that this new attitude brought with it. It was felt not as a release *from* God, but a release *towards* a fuller obedience to him. Instead of struggling to force facts to fit the scholastic theories, one's religious obligation was to seek out and accept humbly and obediently whatever facts his creation should offer, ready and eager to have one's preconceived ideas corrected. 'Do not take descriptions of nature on trust: look for yourself' was the watchword of the new movement.

It is important on the other hand to distinguish this *openness to fresh evidence* from the restless spirit of speculation that we can sometimes find even to this day among pseudo-scientific cranks – the sort of people who are forever postulating 'new laws of nature' that will 'overthrow the existing framework of science'. It is true that these people also make a great fuss about 'the need to keep an enquiring mind'. The difference is that, whereas Galileo and his colleagues found their ideas being shifted under the pressure of facts, the crank, all too often, tries to shift facts to square with his speculative ideas. The pressure is all the wrong way! I do not mean, of course, that new ideas in science can be 'read off' the facts in a straightforward or routine way. The process is a complex one involving imagination and insight as well as observation, and we shall look at it more closely in a moment. But the point is that even the great leaps of imagination, by which men like Einstein and Bohr have landed on new ideas in science, were made only because accumulating evidence forced them off the beaten track of thought.

This principle of conservatism – 'Don't jump unless you must' – is a quite fundamental feature of responsible scientific thinking. It is the necessary counterbalance to the scientist's open-mindedness. Absolutely nothing is ruled out by science as 'impossible': true; but any change in the scientific picture of the world must win its way to acceptance on good evidence. It must pass its exams, so to say. If it can, it will be welcomed – at least, in the long run!

Abstraction

The third great feature of the scientific way of thinking also goes back to Galileo and his fellow pioneers. I mean the scientist's habit of concentrating on a few abstract properties like mass or velocity or temperature, which he can recognize in a great variety of situations, and ignoring the hundreds of particular details which at the moment he judges to be irrelevant. I remember from my student days an examination question set by a humorous university lecturer which began, 'A professor of mathematics of mass M is swinging freely on the end of a rope of length L.' As it happened, the head of the department, who was a keen mountaineer, had been in this awkward predicament during the vacation. The joke was, of course, that for present scientific purposes he could be treated simply as nothing more than 'a body of mass M'. His feelings of alarm as he swung on the end of his rope, the colour of his hair, the make of his boots – all these were irrelevant. Any lump having the same mass would serve equally well for the purpose, and would show the same motion.

In this familiar feature lies much of the power of the scientific way of thinking. It often enables a scientist to predict what will happen in a new situation of a kind he has never seen before, provided only that he concentrates on abstract properties in the situation, like mass, velocity and so forth which he *has* come across and studied. The great art of the scientist consists in learning to discover what are the essential abstract features and to recognize features that he has come across before; learning to see situations in terms of essential abstractions; to see them as instances of something more general.

Hypothesis and observation

This brings out another feature of the scientific way of thinking, its *tentativeness*. Reliable though they usually are, the general conclusions of a scientist are never absolutely final. A conclusion starts life as a hypothesis – a kind of intelligent or inspired guess, which cannot be deduced directly from the evidence we have but which strikes us in the light of experience as a likely possibility. To test it, the scientist first works out some of the results he should expect to follow if it were true. This is a *deductive* step. He next devises an experiment – an artificially contrived or selected situation where the consequences of his hypothesis, if it is correct, should show up in as clear a form as possible. Here we have an *observational* step. If he does not see what he expected, he must go back, modify his hypothesis and try again. If he does get the expected result, he may be entitled to say that his hypothesis has been confirmed.

But – and this is the point – this does not mean that his hypothesis has been *proved*. Not at all. The most we can say is that it has *escaped disproof*. It has stuck its neck out, so to speak, and got away with it – so far. Life for most scientific hypotheses tends to be rather a grim struggle, 'nasty, brutish and short', with death never far round the corner. One's only consolation is that, if a hypothesis has run the gauntlet for a reasonable length of time, then anything that replaces it is likely to include it as a special case – in the way that Einstein's theory of gravitation includes Newton's, for example.

Trying to prove a scientific hypothesis, then – and, still more, trying to prove a powerful generalization like Newton's laws – is rather like trying to prove that a haystack does not contain a needle on the basis of a limited number of samples. A single contrary observation could in principle upset your conclusion, while no amount of confirmation can finally prove it. All you can do is to sample and look as carefully as possible, giving the facts a fair chance to disprove your conclusion, so that you can say in the end not only that you have not found a needle, but also that you have good reason to doubt that anyone will. Obviously the more people who have also looked carefully without success, the more confident you become in your conclusion. In other words, *scientific hypotheses gain our confidence not by finding proof but by repeatedly escaping disproof in a fair test.*

Consider a classic example. Newton's three laws of motion are hypothetical descriptions of the way in which any bodies, anywhere, move if free to do so. Until the beginning of this century it would have been true to say that thousands of tests, of all kinds, had failed to upset Newton's generalizations. People's confidence in the so-called laws became so firm that the philosopher Kant wondered whether any alternative might not be literally unthinkable.

And then, 250 years after they were first framed, came shattering evidence that, in at least one case, Newton's hypotheses *had* been disproved. Bodies moving at high speeds needed significantly different laws to describe their motion. As generalizations, then, the Newtonian formulae did not fit all the facts, and would have to be revised. Einstein developed his theory of relativity from a quite different starting-point, and showed that Newton had actually hit on a special case of a more general hypothesis. This hypothesis of Einstein's was not accepted without a struggle; but under the pressure of growing evidence it has now taken the place of Newton's, and in its turn challenges all comers to disprove it.

Statistics

As long as the evidence is sufficiently clear-cut, testing a hypothesis may be a simple matter; but where evidence is scanty, it is not always easy for the scientist to decide when he ought to jump to a new hypothesis. This is where the business of statistics comes in. The statistician's job is to calculate the odds in favour of jumping to a new hypothesis on given evidence – or, if you like, the risk entailed in generalizing from the small sample of happenings we have studied so far. Suppose for example that we are investigating the effect of a fertilizer on the growth of crops. If we try it out on a single plant, and the plant grows tall and hand-some, we may be tempted to give the credit to the fertilizer. But if we are trained in the statistical habit of thought, like good scientists, we shall be more cautious: we shall ask the conservative question: If we had, say, ten thousand plants like this, how many could we expect to grow to this size without any fertilizer? Obviously we can find out only by trying experiments on large numbers of plants – by 'in-creasing the size of our sample', as we say. Until we do, we cannot begin to evaluate the evidence from our single experiment with fertilizer. Even then, we should want to repeat it with many plants, under many different conditions, before we could lay even a modest bet that our result was statistically significant.

Of course there is a lot more than this to the statistical habit of thought; but the point I want to make is that with this kind of training it is only natural that a scientist tends to be happier in making generalizations about large numbers of instances (whether of plants, or atoms, or human beings) than in dealing with isolated cases. Professionally, he likes to think of individuals as 'typical samples of the mass'; and the popular notion of a scientific attitude often includes the idea that 'individuals do not matter'. Perhaps there is a slight temptation for the scientist to carry over this attitude into his everyday dealings with people; but any idea that he is professionally obliged to do so is complete nonsense.

The importance of vulnerability

The idea that scientific statements 'challenge all comers' brings out a further characteristic emphasis in the scientific attitude. Confronted with any statement, a scientist habitually (and reasonably) asks how it could be tested. If he can see no way of making it vulnerable to test, at least in principle, he cannot admit it as a valid scientific statement, whatever else it may be.

This is not arbitrary dogma, but rather a definition of the rules of his particular game. By these rules, the scientist himself is expected deliberately to contrive situations in which his hypothesis has a chance of being disproved. This is not to say that every proper experiment must test a specific hypothesis (as some philosophers of science have claimed); for in the early phases of a new investigation one sometimes has to explore the ground, with a minimum of preconceived notions. But it does mean that our first aim in any experiment is to refine or correct, and not merely to confirm, what we already believe. An experiment is never an aimless prodding of nature. It is addressing a question to nature. An ideal experiment is one with a range of possible outcomes, each one of which, if it happens, will amplify our understanding one way or another and reduce our uncertainty. Whether or not it confirms our present theories matters little by comparison; for it is only as nature contradicts what we believe or goes beyond what we know already that our scientific knowledge grows.

In summary, then, a hypothesis can be thought of as a kind of template: something we hold up against the real thing (by doing an experiment) in order that any differences between the two can give us fresh information. The template 'subtracts out', as it were, what we think we understand already, so that what we do not yet understand sticks out more clearly, telling us what changes to make in our template before the next experiment. As the process goes on, our template should gradually become a better and better working model of the real thing.

So although in theory it may sound as if scientists are disinterested mortals who never mind being proved wrong, in practice they have good reason to be disappointed if a long-trusted assumption breaks down; for in the end their aim is not just to be ever surprised by new facts, but also to consolidate a body of reliable knowledge on which future scientists may build and future technologists rely.

When a hypothesis has survived enough tests, it is liable to find itself called a scientific 'law'. We looked at one example of this in the case of Newton's laws of motion. But the word 'law' here obviously means something quite different from the sort of law the policeman has to enforce. Scientific laws do not *prescribe* what *must* happen; they *describe* what *has* happened. The earth does not go round the sun because Newton's (or Einstein's) law makes it, or tells it to. The earth goes its own way, and the scientific laws are our generalized way of describing how it goes. All that they prescribe are our expectations.

A good deal of muddled thinking in the past could have been avoided if both Christians and non-Christians had kept this distinction clear. Arguments used to rage, for example, over the question whether God could ever 'disobey his own laws' in order to work a miracle, as if a scientific law were a commandment issued by God, instead of just being our description of the pattern he normally follows.[2]

To the scientist who is a Christian, the best reason for his trust in scientific laws is that they describe the activity of a God whom he knows to be utterly trustworthy. He finds it equally reasonable to believe that, if the human situation ever demanded special and unprecedented activity on the part of God, he as a scientist might find that activity very surprising indeed.

[2] See chapter 6.

3. Detachment and involvement

The scientist gets his knowledge of the physical world by a steadily developing process of intelligent guesswork, guided and tested and constantly corrected by observation, mathematical and logical deduction, and critical experiment. We can lump these activities together if we like under the name of 'the scientific method'; as long as that does not give anyone the impression that there is a routine recipe for doing science, as there is a routine method of constructing equilateral triangles. In that sense, there is no 'scientific method'. Routine methods of making mathematical and logical deductions we may learn. But no routine method exists for inventing fruitful hypotheses. This is a creative activity, in which the scientist has to use his imagination and intuition every bit as keenly as any artist. He may learn it as an art. He can never jog through it as a mechanical routine.

It follows from this that to be creative the scientist just cannot remain aloof from his subject. He will make full use of his intuition and imagination only if he believes in his science, and throws himself into the game with the conviction that he can learn something really worthwhile from it. With the enthusiastic example of the founders of modern science before us, I need hardly add that being Christian does not make it harder, but rather gives us all the more reason, to throw ourselves wholeheartedly into scientific research in this spirit.

But there is another side to the picture. What has been said so far could apply equally well if the scientist were alone on a desert island. But of course one of the chief

3   33

marks of the scientific attitude is the value we set on publicly observable and communicable data and on co-operation between fellow-scientists. Anyone could look through Galileo's telescope and see Jupiter's moons for himself (though it must be admitted that Galileo was not the best example of a co-operative scientist!). Even where the event in question is unrepeatable, and only one scientist witnesses it, he must still write his report in a form that could have been substantiated by a fellow-scientist if one had been present. Incommunicable aspects of his experience, however intense they may have been, find no place in the official scientific version.

Detachment

This brings us to a major feature of the scientific attitude and one that we must consider closely because it introduces something of a paradox. The scientist's reason for keeping his private emotions out of the official picture is that, despite his enthusiasm for his subject, he would like to be able to describe the world *as it is* – as it would be *without* him. This leads him to keep himself detached as far as possible from the system he is observing in order not to disturb it. 'Leave me out of it' is his official watchword. The paradox arises because, as we have seen already in chapter 1, we cannot in fact observe a system at all without its being disturbed to some extent. If it is big enough, or if the statements we want to make about it are vague enough, the disturbance may be negligible; but if we ever want to probe to the limit of detail we at once run up against this paradox. In atomic physics, you remember, this means that no observation can tell us the exact position of an electron without leaving us quite uncertain as to its speed, and *vice versa*. In the social sciences we are even more hampered, because it is very hard to observe people in any detail – especially if you want to ask them questions – without their being disturbed from the state in which you found them. We want the views of a 'typical unreflecting citizen', let us say, on some issue or other. So we pick on a victim and ask him some questions. At once, alas, he ceases to be a typical unreflecting citizen, for we have now forced him to reflect on the issue, and to sharpen his thinking into definite answers to definite questions. By trying to observe his state of mind, we have altered it.

But however hard it may be to achieve, detachment remains one of the most characteristic objectives of the scientific attitude. Typically, scientific knowledge is knowledge 'from the outside' – a spectator's knowledge. The scientist does not – or at least has no scientific reason to – deny that there are whole worlds of knowledge of a different sort to be gained by allowing oneself to get personally involved – in relationships between people or in artistic or religious commitment for example – as long as we distinguish it from *scientific* knowledge. Science may indeed help us to understand (from the outside) the psychological mechanisms at work, and may even suggest ways of enabling them to run more smoothly; but if we attempted to carry a scientific attitude of detachment into the relationship itself, we would simply be trying to have our cake and eat it. We cannot make our motto 'leave me out of this' if we want to know what it is like to be 'in'!

We begin to run into this kind of situation even in such a non-experimental discipline as the study of history. A historian who refused to enter imaginatively into the situation he is studying would miss much of the significance of his material. He must, of course, be true to his objective data – the documents he reads, and so forth; but if he were to fail to use the insight he can gain by imagining himself in the position of the people behind them, he would hardly be worthy of the name of historian. In matters of the arts or of religion this is even more obviously the case. In such fields, to stand aloof would be to shut ourselves out from the knowledge we want. If we are interested at all, we just have to recognize that here we will not be able to make the usual scientific distinction between ourselves as observers, and what we observe. We have to become participants, and accept the new kind of personal responsibility that this brings.

35

The official detachment of the scientist affects not only his experimental methods. It also inevitably restricts the kinds of concepts he uses. According to the rules of his game, every term used in a scientific description must be defined from an outside observer's point of view. There is nothing wrong with this rule; in science it is essential; but it does mean that many of the most important questions that concern us as persons cannot even be *asked* in scientific language, let alone be answered scientifically. Most of the questions that the Bible deals with, for example, are questions of this sort.

The 'limitations' of science

People sometimes express this fact by saying that science has certain boundaries or 'limits' and that religion is 'outside' them; but this I think is an unfortunate way of putting it. It always suggests to me a picture of a flat field with a picket fence labelled 'Religion only: science keep out', with a whole crew of scientists on one side of the fence and theologians on the other, and everybody shoving for all they are worth. No, these limitations of science are not limitations of territory. No part of this world of observable events is outside the boundary of scientific study. However little the scientist may make of some of these from his professional standpoint, he is certainly entitled to try. His conclusions, however limited in scope, may be of real help in appropriate circumstances. The limitations will show up rather in the restricted kinds of description his language allows him to make of the events he studies, and the kinds of point he will be obliged to miss (theoretically) in consequence.

To remove any impression that this applies only in esoteric or 'vague and woolly' subjects, I hope I may be forgiven for offering a well-worn illustration which is undeniably down-to-earth. We are all familiar with those big advertising sign-boards that are made up of hundreds of electric lamps, wired to form a running sequence of words – the sort of thing one sees in Piccadilly Circus telling us that 'Bongo is good for you'. Suppose we were to ask an electrician to tell us in his technical language 'what is on the board'. He gives us a long, careful description in electrical terms, so complete that we can understand just why and how each lamp is flashing, and could if we wanted make a perfect copy of the sign from it.

Now suppose that some argumentative person complains that this painstaking description is still incomplete, on the grounds that it has failed to mention the advertisement. What are we to say? Well; in a sense, of course, he is right. There *are* words on the board, and the electrician indeed has not mentioned them. But does this mean that the electrician was not thorough enough, or that there were some parts of the board that were 'outside his boundaries'? Of course not. It would make nonsense to try to improve the electrical description by adding something at the end so that it read, 'What is on the board is so many electric lamps connected thus and so by so many feet of wire and so on – oh, and an advertisement saying "Bongo is good for you".' The electrician's account, in its own terms, is complete. He has in one sense accounted for every object and event on the board. Moreover if one of the lamps should fail to flash properly it is to him, and not the advertiser, that we should turn for an explanation. What he has not accounted for is the thing *as a whole*. But this is outside of his terms of reference; it is not his job. The notion of an 'advertisement' does not appear among the explanatory concepts in his electrical textbooks.

So it is no reproach to the electrician to insist that once we recognize the *advertisement* we have an explanation that 'accounts for' the phenomenon as a whole in a way that his does not. The advertisement is not something left over on the board if we take away all the items in the electrician's list. It is rather the point or significance of what is there – something we find by starting all over again and describing the very same situation in different, but equally justifiable and illuminating categories. If you come to the board prepared to describe it only in electrical terms you will see nothing but lamps and wires. If you come to the very same board with a different state of readiness, prepared to *read* it, you will see the advertisement. There is nothing optional or arbitrary about this. Once you understand the language of each description, what is there to be described in each is a matter of fact.

To me this is a helpful picture of the kind of connection there is between the scientific description of the universe and the Christian description. As a scientist, I have the job of helping to build in scientific language – at the scientific level – as complete a description of the pattern of physical events as I can, regarding no accessible events as exempt from examination. As a Christian, I find that the very same pattern of events can bear an additional and vital significance as part of the activity of God himself.

To sum up, I think we are justified in speaking of the 'limits of science' only in a *methodological* rather than a *territorial* sense. Designed for situations – all situations – from which the observer can remain detached, certain aspects of the scientific approach automatically cease to apply when detachment is impossible. The point I want to stress is that this kind of limitation is *self-imposed*. The scientist professionally has one great aim – to know more and understand more of our mysterious world from a detached spectator's standpoint. But he has to recognize also that there are many aspects of reality which can be known only through becoming involved with them, so that in order to have knowledge of these he is obliged, by his own ruling principle of 'openness to evidence', to give up scientific detachment. All this seems mere common sense; and it is hard to understand how anyone can honestly argue (as some people do still) that their 'scientific conscience' restricts them to evidence that can be publicly demonstrated, even in matters of religion.

Applied to any publicly observable situation from which the scientist can be sufficiently detached, one could say that the scientific attitude at its best is little more than scrupulous honesty and humility carried to their logical conclusion. Respectful interest in the mechanisms of the natural world, eagerness to be corrected by the publicly accessible data of experience, reluctance to jump to new conclusions unless the facts demand it, and care to avoid disturbing the situation; all these are the least that might be expected of an honestly enquiring mind. It is only where scientific detachment would make the necessary data inaccessible that science of its own accord bows itself out, leaving the scientist just as free as anybody else to get involved as a human being in the more personal business of living.

4. 'Nothing–buttery' and other hazards

In previous chapters we have taken stock of the main features of the scientific habit of thought. We noted that the scientist appeals to experience rather than reason or authority as the way to reliable knowledge of the physical world. He insists that conclusions are scientifically valid only if they are vulnerable to experimental test and have survived it. He analyses situations into their abstract properties, in an attitude of detachment. And he tries – generally with outstanding success – to fit the facts of nature against mechanistic models.

In themselves, when applied to the study of physical phenomena, these principles have nothing anti-religious about them. They were developed by deeply religious men. How then have science and the scientific habit of mind come to present such a barrier to religious conviction for so many of our contemporaries? I think the main reason is that, despite all we have said about their self-defined limitations, when principles such as these become a habit of our thought it is only natural to try to apply them to other fields of knowledge; and most statements of theology do not satisfy these scientific criteria at all well.

A scientific conclusion must in principle be vulnerable to experimental test. But if we take a typical theological statement – for example, that 'Christ died in our place to reconcile us to the Father' – the whole idea of testing seems out of place. Even if we stick to assertions which refer directly to events of daily life, such as the statement 'all things work together for good to those who love God', it is really difficult to think of an experimental test which could either confirm or deny them conclusively for an outside observer, however well they may bear the test of experience for the individual Christian.

Then, as we saw, a scientist arrives at his scientific knowledge of a situation by observing it from a distance, keeping himself detached from it as far as possible; but the Christian gospel says that we cannot come to know God by holding ourselves detached from him. It is more like a friendship or a marriage than a laboratory experiment. Again, a scientific belief is groundless unless it rests on human observation, rather than on unquestionable authority; but the Christian faith claims to rest on God's initiative in revealing himself, without which we could know nothing of him. Of course a Christian also claims – or should be able to claim – to know something of God in his own experience, and to have found him as good as his word; but it must still be agreed that the bulk of Christian theology – and the theology of most other religions – *is* offered on authority. It expressly rejects any idea that it could all have been deduced as a result of unaided human observation.

It is evident, then, that anyone who decides to adopt these scientific habits of mind in *all* aspects of his life will not find much to satisfy him in religious doctrine. It is not surprising that, when some scientifically minded philosophers tried it, they turned away from the Christian faith.

Some people – I confess I am one of them – would say that if you transfer these scientific criteria, developed expressly for the detached study of observable physical objects, into the domain of a religion which is concerned with the personal knowledge of God, you do not *discover* a conflict, you *create* one. They would maintain that the religious and the scientific approaches are not rivals but are complementary, each appropriate to an aspect of experience largely ignored by the other. Even if Christianity were true, they would say, you would not expect to make much sense of it if you tried to squeeze it into a scientific mould. This is the counterpart to the protest of the early scientists against trying to squeeze facts of the natural world into Aristotle's philosophical mould; and I think it is thoroughly justified.

Why then, we may ask, are so many people today positively attracted (in the name of Science) to a way of living which treats God as non-existent or irrelevant? There have been people who found godless living attractive before the age of science, of course! But I think there are two features of science itself which have particularly helped in this dismissal of God. The first is its satisfying power of *explanation*. Explanation, in science, consists in analysing an unfamiliar situation into a set of ingredients, like the connection between force, mass and acceleration, with which we are already familiar. It is not, of course, an anti-religious notion; the early philosophers of science like Francis Bacon were clearer about this than many of their successors. Bacon insisted that what he called the 'providential ordering of nature' was all due to God, however successful we might be in tracing the pattern of physical causes in each case. Somehow, though, especially in the eighteenth and nineteenth centuries, both theologians and scientists seem to have lost sight of this; and we find the idea growing up that God was a kind of *alternative* explanation, which you brought in when you could not find a physical one. Once again, the result was inevitable. Each time a disputed gap in the scientific picture of cause and effect was filled in it was thought to be one foothold less for God: 'One up for science!' There was no doubt about it. If you thought of God only as a way of explaining physical events that you could not understand, science was better, more satisfying in every way. Of course it did not have any answers on ultimate topics like the purpose of life, the significance of death and the hereafter; but questions on these topics could be avoided by calling them 'meaningless' – or at least, 'scientifically meaningless'. For any ordinary puzzles, science seemed to have no rival.

Nothing-buttery

But it was not only that religion seemed to be beaten by science at the game of explanation. The impression created by anti-religious apologists was that religious pretensions had been unmasked. Christians believed the world was created by God; Science (with a capital S) showed that 'really' it was 'nothing but' a fortuitous concourse of atoms. Christians thanked God for sending rain and daily bread; Science explained the agricultural cycle as 'nothing but' the workings of an intricate physical mechanism. Christians believed they had direct evidence of God's dealings with them in their daily experience; Science claimed that soon, if not now, this could be reduced to 'nothing but' the running of their psychological machinery. The implication throughout all this was that Religion had been caught cheating, or at least bluffing, and Science was now letting the cat out of the bag.

Let it first be admitted that some Christian apologists, particularly in the eighteenth and nineteenth centuries, had asked for trouble by making 'arguments for the existence of God' out of phenomena that they considered beyond scientific explanation – thereby sharing in and encouraging the mistaken presupposition of their opponents. The most notorious example of this confusion of issues was perhaps the Darwinian controversy, which we shall look at again in the next chapter.

But whatever excuse there may have been for it, the fallacy underlying such arguments is sufficiently pernicious and widespread to deserve an appropriately rude name, and some twenty-five years ago I christened it 'nothing-buttery'. Its current philosophical label is 'ontological reductionism'. Nothing-buttery is characterized by the notion that by reducing any phenomenon to its components you not only explain it, but *explain it away*. You can debunk love, or bravery, or sin for that matter, by finding the psychological or physiological mechanisms underlying the behaviour in question.[1]

Fortunately the mistake in this kind of reasoning is now becoming widely recognized, by non-Christians as well as by Christians. It is illustrated well enough by our example of the advertising sign (chapter 3). No electrician in his

[1] See chapter 7.

senses would take his success in giving a complete explanation (without mentioning the words on the board) as evidence of the non-existence of the advertisement. Correspondingly, no advertiser in his senses would imagine that he must deny the completeness of the electrician's account in order to defend the real presence of his message.

Now of course there are situations in which we do regard a pre-scientific belief as having been debunked by a scientific explanation. The birth of a child with a hare-lip, for example, we would now regard as sufficiently explicable in genetic terms without bringing in the hare that crossed the mother's path! What makes the difference? Why is this not also 'nothing-buttery'?

A good test is to ask whether the admitted story (the birth of the child with a hare-lip, or the flashing of the lamps in a given pattern) would have had to be different if the other story had been different. The hare-lip, geneticists assure us, would have been equally likely to appear whether or not the mother had met a hare; but the pattern of lamp flashes could not have been the same if the message had been different. So whereas the genetic story, traced back in tightly mechanistic terms, would *debunk* the other, the electrician's story, while equally mechanistic, *corroborates* the other, once we know the code. On the other hand, if someone were to claim to read a message in English text at a time when the mechanism was out of order and producing meaningless flashes, *his* story could be debunked, since the electrician's evidence would show no appropriate correlation between the electrical activity and the alleged message.

Ambiguity of 'reductionism'

In order to avoid confusion we must note that the term 'reductionism' is sometimes used for the well-established scientific habit of taking things to bits in order to understand them. Thus chemists seek to understand the behaviour of molecules by analysing them into atomic nuclei and electrons. Biologists seek to understand cell membranes by analysing them into molecules; and so on. In itself this need

44

have no suggestion of nothing-buttery. In biology, for example, it becomes dangerous only if the scientist imagines that *all* questions of biological interest can be stated and handled in the terms of chemistry or of physics. For the truth is that physics and chemistry have no terms for some of the main concepts and problems that interest the biologist.

What are the chemical or physical equivalents of biological 'adaptation', for example? At first sight the answer might seem simple. The chemist or physicist would expect (in principle) to be able to explain what all the atoms and molecules are doing in an animal that is or becomes well adapted to its environment. But does that make 'adaptation' a physical concept? Of course not; indeed for physics as such it is strictly meaningless, in just the same way and for the same reason that the concept of 'advertising' is meaningless for electrical theory. It is defined for an approach from a different angle, so to speak, an approach which in no way denies the validity of the other, but which recognizes aspects that the other misses. If the biologist were compelled to talk only at the level of physics he would be unable even to *pose* his most characteristic problems, let alone to solve them.

It has sometimes been suggested that the difficulty should be resolved by simply adding such biological terms to the dictionary of physics; but this suggestion misses the point. At the risk of labouring the obvious, let us spell out why. It is not that physics lacks a *word* for adaptation: the point is that, given the approach of physics, the *concept* cannot be defined. Physics is our name for a particular way of taking a situation to bits; and once you have reduced a situation to the 'bits' of physics, you no longer have the 'whole' to which the biologist points when he uses such terms as adaptation.

The prestige of science

The second major factor which has tended to put Science in place of God is the great and well-deserved prestige of

45

applied science or technology. By their disciplined pursuit of knowledge-in-detachment, scientists have over the past few centuries gathered a vast and explosively-growing body of knowledge which has never been equalled for its reliability and breadth of application. In a day of anti-pollution and conservation campaigns it is all too easy to underestimate this.

Putting it crudely (in terms that many atheistic propagandists like to use), in a pre-scientific age a man who feared his crops might fail could think of nothing to do but call upon God. His only defence against disease or plague was to pray. So when in due course the plain fact emerged that prayer, considered as a way of getting what you want, was not nearly so effective as scientific fertilizers and antiseptics, it was easy for people to take it as a loss of prestige for Christianity. It can be argued that prayer is not meant to be just a way of getting what you want; and I agree. I should want to say, too, that the scientific discoveries themselves are just as much God's gifts as the crops. But the fact remained that anyone who *was* accustomed to treat God as an accessory resource found that he got better and more consistent results by pinning his hopes on science – and felt better about it, too, because he did not have to beg in order to get them.

Christians responding to statements of this sort by atheists may be tempted to stress the enormous range of hazards against which our science still leaves us defenceless, and to deprecate reliance on purely material resources. But this response, though fair enough and factually and theologically correct, would I think be misleading in the context. It is not because, nor just as long as, we have limits to our resources that we are expected to pray; for it is in and through the resources we have that God normally answers our prayers. 'Give us this day our daily bread' is a petition not only for emergencies, but for every day. Nor have Christians any scriptural warrant for depreciating as such the material prosperity that science has brought – however deplorable may be men's inability or unwillingness to share this out equitably, and their readiness to let it smother their souls to eternal death. If we want to be biblical in our thinking we will have to work hard to rescue the good name of science from the smears it has picked up in this area, and to restore a positive view of it as a pathway to marvellous and potentially invaluable gifts of God, in which he means men to rejoice with thanksgiving.

There is a great deal more one could say, both about the scientific habit of mind and about the way in which people's attitude to religion has been affected by the growth of science; but perhaps this is enough to set the scene. I hope at least that we can feel something of the mood of enthusiasm and cautious but confident optimism which is inspired by the power of science to explain and to control nature; because however much we may disagree with those people who substitute science for God, we shall never understand them unless we can feel *with* them, as I think a Christian should, the genuine satisfaction that scientific progress can bring. If there are snags in a life without God – and if Christianity is true, there are indeed fatal snags – it is still true that biblical religion does not, and does not claim to, rival science as a means of supplying our material desires: it embraces science as an aspect of our obedience to truth; but it is more concerned with *changing* our wants than with giving us what we may start wanting. Failure to appreciate this point underlies much contemporary talk about the 'irrelevance' of Christianity. Christians who have been through this process of having their own priorities changed must surely be able to set the record straight, clearly and lovingly, without abating one whit the joy and wonder inspired by the history of scientific discovery, and the benefits science still offers if applied in humility and compassion.

5. God – or chance?

'I'm sure such a wonderful structure could never have originated by chance. There must have been a designer's mind behind it all.' How often have you heard arguments on science and religion begin in this way? Certainly there are plenty of the kind on paper; and the centenary of the publication of *The Origin of Species* brought a great crop of them out of the limbo of history to meet the amused scrutiny of our unbelieving age.

A whole generation of earnest Christians and honest agnostics lived and died debating just such questions. They were felt to go to the root of the difference between the 'religious' and 'scientific' approaches. It may thus seem almost impertinent to ask, over a century later, whether this feeling – shared so unquestioningly by both sides – was justified. But was it? Is this antithesis between 'God' and 'chance' a genuinely biblical one? If not, Christians have no brief to defend it. But then, what can we make of the evolutionary debate, and its repercussions in so many different fields?

Two kinds of chance

The first clue comes when we realize that two quite different notions are covered by the word 'chance'.

1. In science, it is used as a technical term to mean the *absence of knowledge of causal connections* between events. For instance, the toss of a coin, or the explosion of a radium atom, or the mutation of a gene, are 'chance' events in that for one reason or another no prior event is (or perhaps can

be) known by us to account for them in some particular.

2. In popular usage, however, the word tends to take on a different shade of meaning, as *chaos*, the antithesis of intelligence, – 'blind chance'. It is this metaphysical notion, often virtually personified as an alternative to God, that our grandfathers obviously meant to resist, and that many unbelieving scientists apparently felt bound to defend in the name of 'Science'. It rather looks as if, in the nineteenth-century debates on the role of 'chance' in biology, the two senses of the word became hopelessly confused, so that 'Science' gained (on both sides) the reputation of making metaphysical assertions which no amount of biological fact could ever justify, while the Bible got the reputation (again, alas, on both sides) of denying the validity of a purely technical, and theologically neutral, scientific notion.

The biblical notion of chance

As usual, the Bible itself has clues that ought to have warned us against a confusion of this sort. Chance in the sense of chaos is indeed recognized (Genesis 1 : 2), but only as something banished from the world by God's creative word. Chance in the neutral sense in which we first defined it, however, is accepted in a very different spirit. 'The lot is cast into the lap,' says the book of Proverbs (16 : 33), 'but the decision is wholly from the Lord.' Could there be a clearer indication that God is the Lord of events which in this sense 'happen by chance', just as much as of those that seem orderly to us? It may indeed be easier for us to see God's hand in the obviously orderly pattern; but the Bible at least will not tolerate the idea that he *must* always work in this way. The 'either – or' with which we began (*either* God *or* chance) is simply not the way the Bible relates the two, if we take 'chance' in the first, technical, sense.

The confusion of 'wonder' and 'puzzlement'

Why, then, did some religious leaders feel that they must dispute hypotheses involving chance processes? They were faced by antagonists, many of whom failed to make the distinction we have noted, and who genuinely supposed that, if a scientific hypothesis succeeded in invoking chance (in the technical sense), it would be a way of disposing of God. But instead of arguing against this confusion, theologians (with a few exceptions) were in the forefront in saying exactly the same thing – except that they, of course, argued that this must mean that the biological hypotheses could not succeed.

The first reason we have already seen in the previous chapter. Orthodox apologetics in the eighteenth and nineteenth centuries had come to rely more and more on arguments from design with a rationalistic flavour, which brought God in as the (necessary) missing term in any scientific explanation of the world. Where the Bible invites us to marvel at the existence of the whole world – the bits whose interconnections we see, as well as those we do not understand – these apologists invited the unbeliever to concentrate on the bits he did not understand (especially the natural history of living organisms) as 'proofs' of the existence of the divine designer. Thus the *metaphysical wonder* expressed by biblical writers (*e.g.*, Psalm 8; Romans 1 : 20), which no amount of scientific understanding can remove, became gradually confused with the *physical puzzlement* of the exploring scientist, which it is his whole ambition to reduce. To borrow an obviously limited analogy from Dorothy Sayers[1] it is not the puzzling details of a dramatic play, but the fact that it exists at all, which betokens the existence of its author. The details may allow us to infer, though precariously, something of his character, and even to wish we knew him; but to make proofs of his existence out of certain details of his drama would be to confuse the issue ludicrously.[2]

There is a real need in our day to bring back a proper sense of awe into our attitude to the natural world; to marvel at the sheer wonder of its existence, and not to be

[1] Dorothy Sayers, *The Mind of the Maker* (Methuen, 1941), and *Unpopular Opinions* (Gollancz, 1946).
[2] See also chapter 6.

frightened out of this by any sneaking feeling that it may not be scientifically or intellectually respectable. The truth is that the greatest scientists, whether Christians or not, have never lost this sense of awe. Any idea that science as such seeks to banish wonder and awe is a delusion, born of wishful thinking.

The abuse of evolutionary theory

Christians believe that the whole universe, and our earth in particular, with all that moves on it, continually owes its being to God the Creator. The Bible uses simple yet profound language to tell us this, in both the Old and New Testaments. Again and again we meet the emphasis, not only that God has conceived and made our universe out of nothing, but also that without his continual creative 'upholding' it would cease to be.

The Bible, however, gives us little, if any, indication of the *scientific* processes by which the features of our world have changed in the course of time. Out of the whole picture the first chapter of Genesis picks out a few highlights with the words, 'And God said, "Let there be . . .".' This reserve is perhaps not surprising, for it was certainly not in order to answer scientific questions that the chapter was written, and in any case God has left us plenty of other clues (such as fossils in the rocks) from which to get our scientific answers if we want to. To most scientists today (whether Christian or non-Christian) these clues seem to fit together to indicate a history of many millions of years, during which it looks as if many species of plants and animals changed or evolved into the forms we know today.

This idea, that (as a Christian would put it) God's way of working has been slow and gradual (the bodies of higher animals coming into being through descent with modification from earlier species), is all that should be meant by the term 'evolution' as used in science. In this technical, scientific sense the idea is theologically neutral, and is widely accepted by biologists who are also biblical Christians. Nothing in the Bible rules it out; in fact, despite superficial appearances and popular belief, on this question the Bible is silent. Doubtless the God of truth will expect us to judge this theory, like others, on its own scientific merits; and it is well to remember that, however widely accepted today, it is still a speculation on trial, and liable itself to evolve as time goes on!

Evolutionism

Hardly was it published, however, before this purely scientific idea was seized upon in the interests of atheism and turned into something quite different. Egged on indirectly by their Christian opponents, unbelieving scientists and their camp-followers triumphantly took up the challenge. 'Evolution' began to be invoked in biology apparently as a substitute for God. And if in biology, why not elsewhere? From standing for a technical hypothesis in the same category as (technical) 'chance', the term was rapidly twisted to mean an atheistic *metaphysical* principle, whose invocation could relieve a man of any theological shivers at the spectacle of the universe. Spelt with a capital E, and dishonestly decked in the prestige of the scientific theory of evolution (which in fact gave it no shred of justification) 'Evolutionism' became a name for a whole anti-religious philosophy, in which 'Evolution' played the role of a more or less personal deity, as the 'real force in the universe'.

Faced with such a confusion of issues, it is hardly surprising that some Christians of the last century were induced to direct their fire in the wrong quarter, and to attack the technical theory instead of its philosophical parasite. The technical theory was of course vulnerable at many points; and still is. The needling of well-informed critics could only be for its good. But it was only to be expected that on such technical questions the theologians were not always as competent as their opponents. As a result they frequently came off badly, and the Christian faith suffered disrepute which had nothing whatever to do with the offence of the cross.

To be fair, it must be said that their anti-religious opponents showed at least an equal degree of incompetence and confusion in theological matters. 'Evolutionism' became for many a dogmatic creed, defended as fiercely, as irrationally and as illiberally as that of the most obscurantist religious apologetics.[3]

Now to deny belief in God may be deplorable from the Christian standpoint (Psalm 14 : 1), but it is not necessarily dishonest. What seems thoroughly dishonest in the above manoeuvre, however, was the implication by one anti-religious writer after another that *science* as such was the ground of their *metaphysical* dismissal of God. This idea, which is seen to be patently false as soon as we recognize the neutral character of the scientific notion of chance, may find some excuse in the mistaken attitude of their theological opponents, who for many years were taken in by it and induced to direct their fire in quite the wrong quarter. But the fact that it hangs over in so many popular anti-religious writings even today is more difficult to excuse. The logically complementary character of religious and scientific categories is now commonplace; yet despite the increasing harmony now recognized between the true spirit of science and Christian faith, confusion between the technical theory of evolution and philosophical 'Evolutionism' is still rife, and the old parasite is not dead.

An author of anti-Christian persuasion who is both better known and less insensitive than most is Sir Julian Huxley, and a well-known article of his entitled 'The Evolutionary Vision'[4] may fairly be cited as a present-day example. In it he says: 'In the evolutionary pattern of thought there is no longer either need or room for the supernatural. The earth was not created; it evolved. . . . Evolutionary man can no longer . . . absolve himself from the hard task of meeting his present problems and planning his future by relying on the

---

[3] For an apt comment on 'The illiberalism of the "Liberals"', see R. Hooykaas, *Christian Faith and the Freedom of Science* (Tyndale Press, 1957), p. 8.

[4] In volume III (*Issues in Evolution*, pp. 249–261) of *Evolution after Darwin*, edited by Sol Tax and Charles Callender (University of Chicago Press, 1961).

will of an omniscient, but unfortunately inscrutable, Providence.' Again G. G. Simpson, after showing that (technical) chance could 'account for' biological development, concludes dogmatically: 'Man is the result of a purposeless and materialistic process that did not have him in mind. He was not planned.'[5] Finally, as recently as 1971, we find the distinguished biologist Jacques Monod arguing that 'Pure chance, absolutely free but blind, (is) at the very root of the stupendous edifice of evolution'; and that therefore 'man at last knows (*sic*) that he is alone in the unfeeling immensity of the universe. . . . Neither his destiny nor his duty have been written down.'[6]

Here are all the marks of the confusion outlined above. The evolution of the created order is thought of as an alternative that excludes its having been created; and divine help and Providence are taken as exclusive alternatives to human effort. The argument quite fails to come to grips with the Christian conception of theism as expressed, for example, in the great New Testament injunction: 'Work out your own salvation with fear and trembling; for *God is at work in you*, both to will and to work for his good pleasure' (Philippians 2 : 12). Still more serious, we have here a confusion between technical evolutionary theory and 'the evolutionary pattern of thought', with the inevitable implication (however unintentional) that it is *scientific fact* which leaves 'no . . . room for the supernatual'. The blunt truth, that no scientific fact can say anything either for or against the supernatural, makes such dogmatism hard to distinguish from sheer wishful thinking. Certainly it has no basis in logic.

If pressed on this matter, it may charitably be supposed that Huxley and Simpson and Monod would have been ready to admit that their arguments could not be logically deduced from scientific fact. They may never have meant to imply that they could. Unfortunately, however, their writings and others like them find their way into the hands of thousands of readers who have no opportunity to press them even if they spot the fallacies; and at secondhand these

[5] G. G. Simpson, *The Meaning of Evolution* (Yale, 1949), p. 344.
[6] *Chance and Necessity* (Collins, 1971), pp. 110, 167.

ideas gain still wider currency, especially in the uncritical minds of school children. Christians have here a constructive, if humbling, task of clarification, in which not only the Bible but also the nature of science itself support them as they seek to bring such misrepresentation to an end.

This does not, I think, mean campaigning to have the case against evolutionary biology presented alongside the case for it. That is the business of scientists as such, and must be left to their scientific integrity and judgment. Nor can Christians expect the positive Christian view of scientific discovery to be inculcated explicitly in a purely scientific course. But it would surely be agreed by all that, if the Christian doctrine of creation is mentioned, then children and others should not be taught falsehoods about it. It needs to be made clear to them, as a matter of fact, that God is declared in the Bible to be creatively active and supreme in *every* twist and turn of this great Drama, whether 'chance' or 'law-abiding' in the scientific sense, which he has thought into being by the word of his power (Hebrews 1 : 2–3). It is a theological blunder to speak of his 'designer's mind' as an alternative, rival explanation to what the scientist may technically classify as 'the operation of chance'; or to regard the success of such scientific explanations as discrediting the Bible. Christians might do well to begin by scrutinizing the teaching in current Christian books and periodicals for any lingering signs of the old confusion of issues, taking urgent steps to make any amends required. The idea that the biological theory of evolution supports anti-Christian 'Evolutionism' is false; and it would be a shame for any Christian literature to align itself with atheistic rationalism in continuing to give currency to it. The parasite should be exposed for what it is, leaving Christians more free than anyone else to enjoy following the trail of God-given scientific clues to the past he has created, giving him glory for whatever unfolding picture they reveal.

6. Creation, law and miracle

The story is told of a school on the Scottish border which was being catechized by the minister, and where the teacher was not particularly good at getting the children to learn their catechism. To save face, she had adopted the strategy of having each child learn the answer to just one question, so that whichever one the visiting minister asked, at least one hand should be able to go up in response. The rehearsal went well; but unfortunately, on the day of the visitation, the boy who was down for the first question was missing. So when the minister asked 'Who made you?' there was a stony silence – eventually broken by a small girl at the back: 'Please sir, the boy God made's no' here the day.'

The tale illustrates rather quaintly a certain kind of misconception, still not uncommon, of what Christians mean by speaking of God in relation to the natural world. In the child's wondering mind, one boy in the class was distinguished from all the others by the fact that *God* had made him. She must have wondered what was odd about him! I want to suggest that many of the debates of the last century arose from a similar mistake: because people imagined that if God had anything to do with the events of the natural world, there must be something scientifically odd about them. The trouble was that, as science advanced, there was a steady shrinkage of the class of events that were 'odd' enough for God to be brought in to explain them. The phenomena of 'life' were especially tempting to theologians. Organic matter was at first thought to be a peculiar product of living bodies, and not synthesizable from inorganic. Then the chemists bridged the gap, and 'life' lost some of its mysterious uniqueness – or so it seemed. Later came the great debates, still going on, about the possibility of synthesizing living cells. One can read innumerable arguments of this general sort, on both sides, in which the presupposition was that God came in, if at all, on the periphery, at the edge of our knowledge. Where our scientific structure became frayed and fuzzy at the edges, there (perhaps) was God; and as knowledge crispened and grew, and developed to close the gaps in the structure, the problem of finding room for God seemed to grow continually more embarrassing.

I do not want to stay with this, because I think enough has been said in earlier chapters to make clear that it was a dismal misconception. When the Bible talks about God, it invites our belief in a Being who is not merely on the periphery of our experience, not a kind of extra unknown term which is necessary to complete the equations of the scientists. The essential point made in the Bible, and in a sense, I think, the key to the whole problem of the relation of science to the Christian faith, is that God, and God's activity, come in not only as extras here and there, but everywhere. If God is active in any part of the physical world, he is in all. If the divine activity means anything, then *all* the events of what we call the physical world are dependent on that activity. When the apostle Paul, speaking at Lystra, declares (Acts 14 : 17) that God 'did not leave himself without witness', he points not to inexplicable oddities in nature, but rather to the everyday things we take for granted: ' . . . for he did good and gave you from heaven rains and fruitful seasons, satisfying your hearts with food and gladness'. In this chapter I want to look in more detail at statements such as these, asking what *kind* of claim is here being made. What *sense* does it make? For if we get it wrong, we will continually run into bogus 'problems'; but if we can get it straight, then the way is clear for facing the things the Bible is really concerned with, in a realistic spirit.

Our world and God

How then can we think meaningfully of God as in all events? Does not this just amount to some sort of pious renaming of events without meaning anything at all? The Bible does not seem to think so. We saw earlier how the writer to the Hebrews speaks of God as 'upholding the universe by his word of power'; and there is much more to the same effect. This notion of the divine 'upholding' of our world is, I think, more difficult for us to grasp in our scientific age than it was in earlier times. The scientific habit of thought accustoms us to look for the explanation of any happening in our world in terms of other earlier happenings, which we call the 'cause' or 'causes' of that happening. We find we can form the succession of events into what we call 'causal chains'; and when we have traced the causal chain-mesh which lies behind any particular event we feel with good reason that we have an explanation for it. It is this kind of explanation that gives us power to make successful predictions, and to construct the reliable devices on which our civilization depends.

Now philosophers of science, as we also noted, have their doubts about the rigidity of the links in these causal chains; but I do not want to complicate things with this, because I do not think that the biblical view of the world depends on there being anything loose or odd about those links. So for the sake of argument, let us think ourselves back into the good old days before Heisenberg's uncertainty principle was heard of, when all events in the scientific picture were thought to be, in principle, tightly interlocked in a causal chain-mesh. This will give the sharpest form to our question: What sense can there be of speaking of God as active here, or 'upholding' this whole going show, in which everything already has its 'causes' in terms of earlier events in the show?

An illustration

Every illustration brings with it a crop of possible misunderstandings which counterbalance its usefulness; but there is one that I have used elsewhere[1] which I find exceptionally helpful in this connection. It starts from our familiar experience of watching a scene on a television screen. When we look at the screen of a television tube, there is a sense in which all that is before us can be reduced to a succession of sparks of light. These cohere in such a way that when we look at the thing as an ordinary viewer, we have the visual experience of watching, let us say, a cricket match. Normally, the control of this television screen is vested in some camera pointing at a faraway field, or a ciné film or the like. But this aspect is irrelevant to the purpose of our illustration, and for that reason I would like to complicate things very slightly. Imagine a T.V. screen which an artist could use as a medium; a human artist who, instead of laying down paint on canvas with a brush, lays down a continual pattern of events on a screen, with the aid of some flexible electronic contraption.

Imagine now a scene brought into being by our artist, in which again a cricket match is taking place. If the artist is good at his job, then we, as we watch it, will see a coherent sequence of events: the ball moving through the air in a nearly parabolic arc, and so forth. We will be able, at least in principle, to discover for ourselves some of the laws of motion and laws of behaviour of the world that our artist has invented – or shall we say created. The artist has a coherent idea, he has embodied it in a succession of events, and if he remains faithful to that idea there will run through and through his created world a causal chain-mesh which scientifically-minded observers can discern in the pattern of events. In other words, any event in the created scene should be 'causally explicable' in terms of earlier events. Why did the ball suddenly change its direction? Because of the impact of the bat; and so on. Scientific questions, then, and scientific answers, ought to make sense as applied to events in the scene, as long as its creator wills it to continue thus.

Suppose now that someone were to remind us that the

[1] D. M. MacKay, *Science and Christian Faith Today* (Falcon Press, second edition, 1973).

whole existence of the scene has another explanation; that it is all upheld by, and owes its coherence to the stability of, the creative will of the artist. This information does not at all devalue our science of the created world; it does not even suggest that our science is weak or incomplete, in the sense that there must after all be unsuspected gaps in the causal chain that we will never be able to fill. It is simply pointing out that, whether or not we have finished our scientific explanation, the *existence of the scene as a whole* needs explaining as a separate issue. Whether or not in our eyes it needs explanation, it happens to be a fact that the whole scene has been thought into being and is held in being by the creative artist.

I like this illustration because it brings out so many things that need saying about science in relation to God. I find nothing in what the Bible says about the dependence of our world on God to suggest that this dependence should be demonstrable by some scientific peculiarity of its past or present behaviour. That would be as odd as to suggest that the existence of the artist could be detected by taking a look at some peculiarity of a corner of the cricket field. It would just obscure the point; for his existence is demonstrated no less and no more by the parts of the scene we have learnt to understand by our science. Indeed, unless the artist chooses to do something deliberately to reveal it, his existence need never logically be suspected from any particular feature of the scene he has created. He is not one of the *objects* in the world that he has thought into being. He as creator is not 'in the same world' as the cricket team. So it would be absurd to suggest that scientific analysis of the events of the cricket field must eventually lead to something scientifically inexplicable, just because the scene is dependent on the artist for its existence. By the same token, any idea that God's being active in our world means that there must be 'something science can't explain' – about living bodies, or interstellar hydrogen, or whatever – is a complete *non sequitur*. The laws of nature we discover are not *alternatives* to divine activity, but only our *codification* of that activity in its normal manifestations.

Two questions of origins

If this is at all a fair illustration of what the Bible is saying, you can see why I suggested that we ought to take a fresh look at some of the old controversies. Take for example the question of origins. The point that our illustration brings out is that there are two quite different senses in which we can speak of the origin of the world. In the case of the cricket match, one question we could ask is: 'Who is holding this scene in being? Whose idea is it? In whose mind did it originate?' In this sense we would not be asking about any particular happenings in the past of the created world, but rather about the creative activity of the author's mind, by virtue of which the whole going show (past, present, future) has been conceived into existence.

Alternatively, we might mean: 'How does this whole story begin? Is there a unique starting-point in the past from which everything unfolds?' This would be a question about the origin of the artist's created world in a scientific sense, which might be answered, for example, by saying, 'Well, if you were to extrapolate back so many hours, or so many centuries, or so many millions of years, you would come to such and such initial causes *within* the created world.' Indeed, if the creative artist had conceived things appropriately, we might find all our clues pointing back to one particular singular point in time as the (scientific) 'origin' of the created world in the cosmologist's sense. On the other hand, if the artist conceived his world differently, this business of going back by scientific inference from the present into the past might never lead us to a unique starting-point. If it did not, we might be driven to a theory of an 'infinite past' for the created world that we were studying. In neither case, however, would any conclusions as to the origin of the created world in this sense throw any doubt on the origin of the whole going show in the creative mind of the artist. To create a world with an 'infinite past' would not involve him in any greater difficulty than to create one whose inferable past was finite.

Similarly, if we ask about the origin of our own world, we

may mean one of two different questions: either 'Where does our whole drama come from? How come there is such a drama at all?' or alternatively, 'How did our world story begin, in the depths of time and space? What was the first event in the drama?' I think it is fair to say that the Bible's concern, first and foremost, and from start to finish, is with the *first* of these questions. It is urging us to recognize that, whatever our success in looking for the causal chains that link the past and present events of our world, there is quite another question that needs to be asked, or rather (it would say) another fact that needs to be faced: namely, that our whole ongoing universe owes its existence, and its point and purpose, to the continuing stability of the creative will of God.

If that is at all a true picture of what biblical theism means by the createdness of our world then, of course, any argument whether the past, which is scientifically inferred from the present, is an 'evolutionary' past, or a past that goes back to a big bang, or a past of continuous creation, is irrelevant to the claim that the Bible makes, namely that, whatever the actual form of the past, it is God's idea, and it is God who thought into being and continues to hold in being the world in which we find ourselves.

Miracles

The second of the areas of debate illuminated by this illustration is the question of miracles. By this I do not mean the *historical* question whether particular events actually happened in such a way as to break the usual chain-mesh of cause and effect, but rather the philosophical question of the *possibility* of such events in a world such as ours, since it is in this connection that the claim is often made that science leaves no room for God. The point immediately suggested by our illustration is that this question needs to be turned the other way around. In the humanly 'created' world, if the artist has continually to give being to each successive moment, then what might seem surprising is not the appearance of anything out of the ordinary on the screen, but the fact that extraordinary things do not happen more often. It is just this that betokens the stability and the competence and the coherence of the artist's conception.

Similarly from the theistic point of view, the question we ought to be asking about God's created world is not 'How could miracles happen?', but 'How come the world is as regular as it is?' 'Why should the pattern of events be as dependable as it is?' The Bible answers this in terms of the personal faithfulness of God; but our illustration makes it clear that, if it were God's will to bring about a happening quite out of the ordinary run, he would have no more difficulty in doing so than our artist would if he wanted to change the scene on the screen. What the Bible is always saying is that God normally maintains our world according to its regular pattern, as part of a coherent plan: one aspect of the way he has determined that his whole drama shall run. It is just this that the Bible advances as its guarantee of our day-to-day expectations, whether as scientists or as ordinary mortals. God, as the Bible portrays him, has a coherent purpose. He is not capricious, and therefore we can trust him not to fool us; it is consistent with his purpose to make tomorrow normally according to the pattern of today.

One obvious imperfection in our illustration must be noted at this point. It might seem to suggest that as the human artist is quite outside the world he creates, and so quite unknowable by the characters in it, so God, even if we acknowledge him as our Creator, must be unknowable by us and in that sense irrelevant to us. What the Bible declares, however, is that part of God's purpose of faithfulness to us is to confront us personally, and to deal personally with the problems which we each have (whether we know it or not) at the spiritual level.[2] This over-all purpose has required God to address us in history, and to project himself personally into his drama (something without parallel in our illustration). If this is true, then of course our scientific study of the normal pattern of events cannot tell us what to expect on such special occasions; and it would

[2] See chapter 10.

in a sense be more surprising if the normal pattern were *not* superseded.

Once we understand the kind of claim the Bible is making about the everyday dependence of our world on God, then, there is no 'problem of miracle' in the sense of a conflict between our scientific knowledge and the belief that miracles could happen. What we are encouraged to ask rather is in what way the historical events that Christians call miraculous have expressed this faithfulness of God. The Bible does not encourage a belief in events totally without rationale from God's standpoint. The biblical claim is that wherever God did 'work' or 'bring into being' an event which we call a miracle, whether or not it broke with scientific precedent, he did it because in the over-all pattern of his drama it made *more* sense at that point: because his total plan and purpose for our world would have been *less* coherent had it not occurred in the way it did.

The clearest evidence of this principle of 'higher level rationality' as applied to miracles is the Bible's attitude to the resurrection of Christ. First-century people had no need of our modern biological knowledge in order to find the idea of resurrection incredible in terms of normal precedent; yet in Peter's first recorded sermon (Acts 2 : 24) he speaks of the resurrection of Christ not as inexplicable but as *inevitable*. He says that God raised him up and delivered him from death 'because it was not possible for him to be held by it'. In other words, it would not have made sense for the Creator, when he came into his own drama, to have been destroyed in any ultimate sense by characters in that drama. So the suggestion I am making is, I think, fair to the spirit as well as to the letter of the Bible: namely that we shall see the concept of miracle as intellectually embarrassing only if we misconceive the nature of the day-to-day dependence claimed for our world upon God; but that this does not mean that the Bible gives us a licence to believe in ultimate disorder. Rather on the contrary, biblical theism insists that any breaks with scientific precedent that have occurred were but a further expression of the same faithfulness to a coherent over-all purpose which is normally expressed in the day-to-day reliability of nature on which we depend as scientists.

So in answer to the question, 'Does science leave room for the idea of God?' I want to say not just that there is room of the right kind, but that the biblical doctrine of nature suggests a positive harmony between the scientific analysis of the natural world and its divine significance, as God's 'idea' embodied in the events we study as scientists. Here is a positive incentive for the scientist, for his guarantee is not the impersonal reliability of a machine, but the personal faithfulness of a God whose creatures we are, and who has shown us his trustworthy character in the life of Jesus Christ. If the scientist is also a Christian, there is no implication that he should necessarily do better in science, still less that his scientific findings should differ from those of his non-Christian colleagues; but it is clear that he has if anything a firmer ground for his conviction and enthusiasm as a scientist. The fears expressed by some unbelievers, that to accept the possibility of miracle in the biblical sense would make nonsense of the whole scientific enterprise, are fundamentally groundless.

5

7. Christian and Scientific ideas of man[1]

The biblical doctrine of man is all-embracing. It begins with the declaration that he, like the rest of his world, is created; and that he is created 'ensouled' and for a purpose. The whole point of his existence consists in the possibility of his forming and living out a loving, dependent and obedient relationship with his own Creator, as of a son with a father: this relationship being expressed in and through his response to the daily opportunities offered by the world of people and things. It goes on to assert, however, that he is not only unworthy of this relationship, by nature he is not even keen on it. He would rather not 'have God in his knowledge' (at least not in *all* his knowledge, in the intimate sense that the Hebrews gave to the word); in short he is a fallen sinner. Yet in all this the Bible from start to finish presents man as a responsible being, who is indeed responsible for his disgrace in the eyes of his Maker.

The burden of the biblical message, however, is not doom but hope. Man is redeemable: redeemable not in his own strength, but by virtue of what God has taken the initiative to do for him, in coming among us in Christ, in dying and rising again for our redemption to eternal life. Eternal life, then, is the culmination of the Bible's picture of our nature and destiny.

I have begun with these 'headlines' from Christian teaching because I think that each of them is a potential

---

[1] The argument of this chapter and the next may not be easy to follow at a first reading. I have therefore included a brief Appendix (pp. 106 ff) in which I have tried to deal with the objections most commonly raised when I have spoken on this subject.

point of contact (and if we are not clear in our minds as to what Scripture is saying, a potential point of conflict) with the scientific picture of man as it is gradually beginning to build up. On the other hand I hope that anyone who expects this chapter to concentrate on the latest developments in the science of man will not feel too disappointed if it does not do so. One could indeed write at great length on the new insights into the mechanisms of the brain that have been gained from the standpoint of communication engineering, and the exciting prospects of interdisciplinary brain research at the present time. But for our present purpose I do not think that this kind of progress report is necessary. The argument of this chapter and the next will be that particular details of what science has achieved so far in its mechanistic understanding of man, at the various levels of physiology, psychology, psychoanalysis and so on, in principle leave untouched the validity of what the Bible has to say about him. To clarify the issue, therefore, I suggest we begin by imagining ourselves projected forward to a time when (for the sake of argument) we may suppose that the scientific enterprise has been crowned with success. By 'the scientific enterprise' I want to denote all attempts to understand man as a phenomenon in causal terms: in terms of physical chemistry at one level, physiology at another, psychology at another, psychoanalysis at another. Imagine that this multiple onslaught on the problem of understanding man as a behaving system has completely succeeded. Suppose we had all the answers to the questions we might like to ask as physicists, physiologists and so forth about human behaviour, viewed in the small or in the large. What then? What I hope to show is that in fact, even if this enterprise were completed, the scriptural doctrines which I have just mentioned would stand as strongly as ever before; and that therefore it is quite pointless for those who may be Christians but not scientists to be anxiously scanning the newspapers for the latest discovery in the science of the brain, or whatever, afraid that it might embarrass our Christian faith. In other words, though this may involve us in some tough thinking, I want to suggest

67

that if we think biblically and clearly our minds can be freed from a great deal of unnecessary extrapolation and speculation, in order to concentrate on constructive relationships between our growing scientific understanding and the biblical doctrine of man.

The createdness of man

To bring out the underlying principles it may be best to concentrate on one or two main areas in which we need to keep our thinking clear if we are to avoid mistaken conflicts with mechanistic science as applied to man. The first concerns the *createdness* of man. This alone could require a painful and detailed backtracking over arguments of the past centuries to do it justice, and we have touched on it in earlier chapters. Let me just say that as I read the scriptural doctrine of creation, illuminated not only by the familiar passages in Genesis but also by such New Testament passages as Colossians 1 : 16, 17, and Hebrews 1 : 3, I think the danger is not that we take too high a view of God as Creator, but that our view is too low. Here I have found further help in the illustration we considered in chapter 6 – the idea of the creative imagination of an artist, or novelist or dramatist. The analogy, of course, is imperfect, but it can, I think, help to clear our minds of false and low views of God as Creator if we look first at the kind of relationship that exists between, let us say, Hamlet and Shakespeare.

We know what we mean by saying that Hamlet is Shakespeare's creation. We mean that it is only because Shakespeare's creative imagination worked constructively and said 'Let us have someone called Hamlet in such and such an environment' that the drama of Hamlet took form. Of course we recognize the differences that exist between Shakespeare, a merely human creator, and God. For one thing, whereas what Shakespeare imagines takes only mental form, what God imagines when he says 'let there be' can take physical form in our world. On one point at least, however, I think that the parallel is exact. Shakespeare, in order to create Hamlet, has had to think about Hamlet individually. If he had not done so there would not have been any Hamlet. How many million other beings may exist in Hamlet's world, how vast it is, what sort of natural history preceded his appearance, what ancestors he had, and so forth – none of these questions affect the facts (a) that Shakespeare is the creator of Hamlet, and (b) that Hamlet is individually known to Shakespeare.

The basic point is one we have met before.[2] If we take seriously what the Bible means by creation we see that it is not just a single datable event, which happened at a particular point in time; it is rather a continuing relationship of dependence between us and God, such that the whole of our drama, its past, its present and its future, owes its form and its ongoing existence, moment by moment, to his creative power. As soon as we see this, I think it becomes clear that questions of the size of the universe, for instance, are utterly irrelevant to the biblical teaching that God knows each one of us individually, and cares for and about us. The familiar argument, that 'the universe is too vast, and man too tiny' for God to be interested in us, would be relevant only if God were one of the features *in* his universe; but the Bible puts it the other way round. It is the whole universe which is *in him*; and God's knowledge of us as individuals is as unaffected by the vastness of the setting which he has created along with us, as Shakespeare's knowledge of Hamlet is unaffected by the vastness of the land of Denmark. It is totally irrelevant.

By the same token (as I have suggested in chapter 5) arguments about the evolution of man's body seem to be equally irrelevant to the biblical view of man as God's creation, and of man's responsibility and significance in the eyes of God. We will come back to that point; meantime I commend this image (of Hamlet and Shakespeare) just as a 'loosener', to help in getting rid of false ideas of possible conflict between scientific discoveries and biblical doctrine. If God creates the whole of our drama – its past, its present and its future – it is not at all surprising if when we study

[2] See chapter 6.

69

man's past scientifically we find it a coherent whole at the levels of biology and physics.

The soul

Secondly, what about the concept of the soul? The early passages in the Bible say that man 'became a living soul' (AV). I think the word 'became' is important. A living soul, or as the RSV puts it 'a living being', is something we *become*. The Hebrew word for 'soul' here is *nephesh*, which we **are** told could well be translated 'organism', or perhaps **'mind**-body'. It is also used of lower animals. What I want to suggest is that there are no grounds for the notion that the Bible teaches that man's body is like a kind of chariot, or a motor car with controls which must be 'open ended' for something non-physical to influence them. If we start with that sort of presupposition I think we get into trouble not only with mechanistic physiology, but also with Scripture itself. There are indeed some biblical passages in pictorial language which might, if we were unguarded, lead us into thinking in this way. But the Bible, as it so often does, corrects any attempt to take these as teaching science by offering us a variety of quite different images. It speaks for example of man as 'clothed' with his body, and of our 'inhabiting' it as a tent; but more often the distinction it draws is between our 'mortal body' and the 'glorious body' which is promised in the resurrection. Man here is viewed as a *unity* of mind-and-body, or better, as *mind-embodied*. Such images offer no justification for expecting any parts of the chain-mesh of cause and effect in the brain to have 'loose ends'.

But, it may be asked, if that chain-mesh were complete, would not this mean that man is nothing more than a machine, or at least that all idea of responsibility is eliminated? These are indeed key questions which we must consider in a moment; but let me say at once that I think they imply false extrapolations from what the Bible has to say. The Bible insists both that man is responsible and that he is 'dust'. As dust he has continuity with the natural physical order. As *nephesh*, organism, mind-body, he has continuity with the animal kingdom. Finally, the Bible goes on to speak of yet a third aspect of our nature. Man is capable of 'eternal life'. He is by nature spiritually dead; but he can be made alive to eternal life, and enjoy resurrection from the dead. I shall argue that none of these claims contains any suggestion that the scientist cannot succeed in his attempt to understand the body as a mechanism.

Man a machine?

Let us first look more closely at the question, 'Is man nothing but a machine?' It is fair to note at the outset that no answer is possible which would deny that you, who ask the question, are a conscious being; for the question could not have arisen if you were not, nor would there be any point in answering you. But we have no need to rest our case on this argument, although I think it has considerable force.[3] The point I want to make is that the phrase 'nothing but', here as elsewhere, is ambiguous; and that once the ambiguity is resolved along the lines developed in chapter 4, the sting in the question is drawn. Nobody objects to the claim that an advertising sign is 'nothing but lamps on a board', unless the claimant imagines that on this account he has debunked it.

Perhaps one or two more examples may help to bring out the generality of this point, and the foolishness of the 'nothing-buttery' that denies it. A sign on the wall saying 'No smoking' is easily shown to be 'nothing but' ink on card; but if anyone thinks this will excuse him from observing it, the usher will soon show him differently. When he claims that what is on the card is 'nothing but ink' he is telling the truth in a certain simple, literal sense. But if he means it has therefore no claim on his attention as a message (in fact a prohibition) he is talking nonsense. The phrase 'nothing but' all too often betokens an attempt to *obscure the point* of a situation that makes an inconvenient claim.

[3] See chapter 9.

Take another illustration. A mathematician, or a business man, sets up a problem on a computer; the electronic wheels turn, and eventually out comes a typed message. Now it is not unknown for problems to be badly set up, so that instead of producing the answer, the machine goes into some kind of oscillation, or an endless cycle of activity. Suppose we ask the electronic engineer to explain what is happening. He traces the electric current through all the transistors and so forth in the computer, and in purely electrical terms, without any reference to the problem set up, he explains all the events before us. Now suppose the mathematician says, 'Wait a moment; I can see what is wrong. The real explanation is that we have made a mistake in the programme.' Does this *conflict* with what the electronic engineer has said? Not at all. The mathematician is merely saying that when the engineer has finished telling his story, there is another to be told, which reveals the mathematical point or significance of the situation. Had the trouble been due to an electrical fault, of course, the boot would have been on the other foot. The important point is that, in general, there is not only room but *need* for stories of both kinds to be true at the same time. What we have to ask is not which story is true, but which story is relevant in a particular context.

As we saw in chapter 4, the 'nothing-buttery' assumption – that when you have verified a complete account in one set of terms you automatically debunk any others – is simply mistaken in logic. Often, indeed, it is an example of wishful thinking (or wishful 'unthinking'). Anyone who tries to apply this to man, by arguing that a full explanation of man's brain in mechanistic terms would debunk man's spiritual nature, is dropping a logical brick. Notice, however, that this does not mean that there *must* be truth in the biblical account; it means only that the biblical account is not *disproved* by any amount of mechanical explanation in terms of physics, chemistry, information engineering or what have you. By the same token, I would argue that Christians as such have no justification in Scripture for postulating any sort of barrier to the progress of brain science. 'Physical', 'mental' and 'spiritual' are complementary categories, all of which are embraced by the totality of what it is to be a man.

'Nothing but' an animal?

We must consider another kind of objection, however, based on what I might call the thin-end-of-the-wedge argument, or the argument from continuity. Are we not saying that, on this assumption, man is, if not 'nothing but' a machine, watch the phrase, 'nothing but'. We might mean simply that by taking a man's brain apart we could find the same kind of 'works' that we would find in the brains of lower animals. That seems to me unobjectionable. The 'thin-end-of-the-wedge' argument, however, would be that, if we imagine a series of animal brains of increasing complexity ending with that of man, we would have to admit that man is indistinguishable in essence from lower animals. This simply does not follow. It is like arguing that if we cannot define sharply how many hairs make a beard, then a clean-shaven chin is indistinguishable from a bearded one.

Of course, it is fair to point out that the genetic mechanisms of reproduction make it extremely improbable that there could be complete continuity of species all the way down from man. Mutations, or discontinuous changes in the genetic specification, seem to be necessary if large changes are to take place in the progeny of a given species. The bigger the change, the bigger the probability that it will involve a discrete jump (or more than one) in the specification. So it is perhaps not realistic even to imagine a continuity of types of brain all the way down from man. Nevertheless, just to clear our minds, let us imagine that there were such a continuity. I want to argue that even then, the distinction between man and other animals would be in no way obliterated.

Let me show what I mean by yet another simple illustration. If we give a child a box with five hundred letters of the alphabet, he can use them to make up sentences, statements which may be true or false, and so on. We have equipped him with a means of communication. Suppose now that, one by one, we reduce the number of letters until he ends up with just two. In one sense there is *continuity* between what he now has, and the original set of 500 letters. Yet equally clearly there is a *qualitative difference* between what is possible with 500 letters and what is possible with two letters, a distinction which no thin-end-of-the-wedge argument gets rid of. There will in fact be a particular 'critical size' of kit below which no sentence can be constructed at all.

Or again, suppose we feed gas to a burner, and mix air with it. If we mix too much air with the gas and hold a glowing splint over the burner, it will not light. Gradually increasing the proportion of gas to air – a continuous process – we will reach a point at which, suddenly, a flame appears – a qualitatively new phenomenon. Once again we see that to discover (or postulate) a continuous transition between one extreme and another does not for a moment rule out the possibility of qualitatively new phenomena distinguishing one extreme from the other. The Christian belief that man differs qualitatively and essentially from other animals need imply nothing one way or the other about the continuity of his brain-development with that of lower animals.

Eternal life

Finally under the heading of Christian and scientific ideas of man, what of the biblical doctrine of resurrection to eternal life? Does our view of the unity of mind and body make this more difficult to take seriously today? I think not. Indeed, I suggest that the illustrations we have already used make this particularly clear. Take the case of a message chalked on a blackboard. To clear the board, we rub the surface until we are left with a handful of chalk. As far as that board is concerned the message is gone. But of course if tomorrow we, the originators, want to express the same message again, here or elsewhere, we have no difficulty in doing so. It is not necessary for us to use the original chalk, or even to use chalk at all. What matters is the arrangement of the chalk in which the message was embodied; and it is entirely up to us whether its new embodiment uses the same or different material, or indeed whether it is expressed in some utterly new medium (such as speech, for example), which is recognizably the same only in some essential aspect. Again, if a computer operating a given programme were to catch fire and be destroyed, we would certainly say that that was the end of that particular embodiment of the programme. But if we wanted that same programme to run in a fresh embodiment, it would be quite unnecessary to salvage the original computer parts or even to replicate the original mechanism. Any active medium (even operations with paper-and-pencil) which gave expression to the same structure and sequence of relationships could in principle embody the very same programme.

If, then, our human personality is related to our bodies in anything like the way that a message or a computer programme is related to its embodiments, it is clear that brain science has absolutely nothing to say against the possibility of eternal life. If it is God's will that, although these bodies of ours have been rubbed off the scene, we shall nevertheless be re-embodied in the world to come, this possibility in no way conflicts with our scientific knowledge. There is nothing in the scriptural doctrine of the resurrection of the body which suggests that, as scientists, we should be frustrated in looking for purely mechanistic explanations of bodily behaviour.

8. Freedom and responsibility[1]

Our argument has so far been that personal and spiritual categories are not ruled out by mechanistic explanations of human behaviour. These categories could be just as valid as ever they were, even if we imagined that at the physical level our brains were as mechanical as a cash register. But now it is time to face the question of our freedom and responsibility. Would not all this mean that just as we do not hold a cash register responsible for its actions, so we could not hold a man responsible for his? What about the concept of sin? Would not sin be reduced to a purely natural phenomenon?

Let us begin at the theological end, and see what the Bible means by responsibility. Basically, it means answer-ability-to-God. Here we notice a vital difference between our situation and that of Hamlet *vis-à-vis* Shakespeare, which we considered in the previous chapter. Shakespeare was a mere man: Hamlet never knew Shakespeare, and could not know Shakespeare. What makes our situation different, according to the Bible and Christian experience, is that in our world the Creator has taken the initiative to make himself knowable, by projecting himself into his creation as one of the agents in it. He has done so both uniquely and focally in the person and life and work of Christ, and continually in the agency of his Spirit. Since, then, God is one of the agents of his own drama, we are able in principle not only to know him, but also to say yes and

[1] As with chapter 7 the argument of this chapter may not be easy to follow at a first reading. Some of the objections most commonly raised are dealt with briefly in the Appendix (pp. 106 ff.).

no to him; for he addresses us as responsible beings, and he invites us into a fellowship with himself which will ultimately cost us the last relic of our own self-centredness.

Sin

It is here, of course, that the concept of sin comes in. Not only are we unfit for such fellowship, we are *unwilling* for it; and it is our unwillingness which is our sin. This must be clearly distinguished from our *sins*, which are the particular symptoms in our lives showing that we are 'out of gear' with the Creator who meets us day by day with the question, 'Who is to be master?' Sins, then, are the natural outcome of this broken relationship; and this incidentally is quite in line with what the psychologist would say about the 'naturalness' of such human antisocial behaviour. It *is* natural for us to commit sins: that is our trouble. We have what is called a fallen nature. It would be a great mistake for Christians to try to argue that there cannot be a psychological explanation of sins. All of these events in our personality, I am prepared to believe, can in principle have their psychological explanation, because man is a unity, and such an explanation merely works out in technical terms what follows from the biblical assertion that our nature is fallen. According to the Bible, ours is a unity which is radically out of gear with the mind of God – unless and until God takes the initiative in rectifying the break. So I suggest that the 'naturalness' which the psychologist finds in what the Bible calls sins is something that should encourage the scientist, and particularly the psychologist of religion, to go ahead and expect to find psychological correlates of our fallenness. The curse on the natural order, which we experience in so many diverse ways in suffering and frustration as well as in temptation, is a curse on the whole fabric of it, and therefore on our own bodily machinery as a part of it. We can only expect our personalities as expressed in and through those bodies to be also under the curse. Perhaps this personal way in which the curse of the Fall manifests itself is close to what theologians mean by 'original sin'. But I have no wish to indulge in speculation. All I am suggesting is that we must not divorce ourselves as creatures from the rest of the natural order, and we need not expect the curse on the whole natural order to leave our bodily machinery unaffected.

Responsibility

But what about this question of responsibility? When I face a choice which concerns my attitude to God, could not some super-scientist in principle write down a prediction of what the choice would be? If so, am I not bound to fulfil it? How then can I bear responsibility for it? If our brains were as mechanical as cash registers, then surely before we made any choice the outcome would be already fixed and inevitable, if only we knew it?

This sounds a strong argument, and it has been implicitly accepted by many people on both sides of the traditional debate over 'free will'. I believe that it contains a logical fallacy. When examined closely, the argument turns out to be invalid for reasons which have nothing to do with the pros and cons of determinism as a *physical theory*. In order to make this clear, let us see what would (and what would not) follow if knowledge of our brain mechanisms and the forces acting on and in them *were* sufficient to allow our actions to be predicted (secretly) by a detached observer. In practice, this may be utterly impossible; but in principle it is conceivable that someone who knew what all our brain cells were doing, and all the outside influences that would be exerted on them, could successfully predict *secretly* the outcome of a decision we have not yet made. Let us suppose for the sake of argument that he could, and did. 'Wait and see', he might say. 'I won't tell you my prediction now, but you will find in due course that I am right.' After we have made our decision, he produces recorded evidence showing that he indeed knew what we would do before we did it. Would this predictive knowledge of his prove that the outcome was all along inevitable for us, if only we had known it?

Oddly enough, it would not – though we shall have to think carefully to see why. It would admittedly show that the outcome was predictable (and in *that* sense 'inevitable') *from the standpoint of the detached observer*. But before he could claim that it was also *inevitable for you* he would have to show that this is also the outcome that *you* would have been correct to accept as inevitable, if only you had known it. Unfortunately for him, this does not follow! The basic point is that (according to mechanistic brain theory itself) what you believe, accept as inevitable, *etc.*, is represented in some precise sense by the state of your brain. Thus no completely detailed description of the present or immediately future state of your brain could be equally accurate whether or not you believed it. If it were accurate before you believed it, then when you believed it your brain-state must change in some respect, so that the description must be out of date and you would be in error to believe it. Suppose on the other hand that it were cunningly adjusted to allow for the brain-effects (or more precisely, the brain-correlates) of your believing it, so that if and only if you believed it the changes in your brain would make it correct. Then if you were not to believe it you would not be in error, since in that case your brain would not be in the state described or implied.

In short, the present and immediately future state of your brain, however predictable by a detached observer, has *no completely determinate specification* that *you* would be unconditionally correct to accept, and in error to reject, if only you knew it. In that sense, your immediate future is not inevitable for you. To put it otherwise, no completely detailed specification of your immediate future can exist, upon which both you and all observers would be correct to agree, until after the event. The observer's data, even if he shared them with you afterwards, would only confirm this peculiar logical fact about the situation at the time you made your choice, the fact that it was 'logically indeterminate'.[2]

Notice that we are not claiming that *all* descriptions of

[2] See references listed at the end of this chapter.

your future are indeterminate in this sense. A description of a brain-state which is vague enough, or sufficiently far in the future, or sufficiently unrelated to the parts of your brain that would be affected by your believing it, may have as good (or almost as good) a claim to your assent as to that of a detached observer. A prediction that you will decide to eat and drink at some time within the next month for example, or that your heart-rate is about to increase, might not be significantly invalidated if you knew of it and believed it. Moreover there may be some future actions, such as paying a debt, which you have already decided to take, and would not wish to alter even though they were predicted to you.

The question in every case is not whether you can believe the prediction if you wish to, but whether it has an un-conditional claim to your assent. Would you be in error to disbelieve it, whether you like it or not, if only you knew it? If not, then the action predicted is not inevitable for you.

Coming back to our super-scientist with his piece of paper, I hope it is now clear that the prediction he has written on it is binding only upon him, and not at all upon you. Even if nobody tells you of it, the prediction is self-disqualified from any unconditional claim to your assent. Your accepting any such specification beforehand would inevitably upset the basis on which it is calculated, for it would amount to making up your mind in advance of the point at which it described you as doing so! The important question, then, is not 'Is the *predictor* correct in believing what he has written on that piece of paper?', but 'Would I be correct to believe (and mistaken to disbelieve) what is written on that piece of paper, as fixed and inevitable, if only I knew it?'. *He* may well be correct to believe it, and mistaken to disbelieve it, provided he can keep it to himself. What he cannot claim is that *you* would be.

Let me summarize the argument. Paradoxical though it may seem, it would clearly be self-contradictory for you to believe certain things that a detached observer can correctly say (behind your back) about your future. It is not that what he says of you is false, but rather that for you it is nonsense. It would not be possible for you to be the person he is describing if you were to believe his description of a decision that you have not yet taken. Thus you and I, even if our brains were as mechanical as clockwork, would be mistaken to believe that there exists, unknown to us, any complete prediction of a choice we have not yet made, which we would be correct to accept as inevitable if only we knew it. To put it the other way round, no prediction of a future choice can exist which is already and for all time binding upon you, whether you like it or not, if only you knew it. In this sense your future, in at least some details, is logically indeterminate. No matter how predictable it may be for others, a normal choice is still a situation whose outcome is *up to you*. Unless you make it, it will not be made; and the way you make it will determine the outcome. You cannot be denied responsibility for it afterwards on the grounds that it was predictable by detached observers; for the same evidence that shows that they were justified in *their* expectations would show also that *you* would have been in error to share their view.

Predestination

This may sound strange to those of us who have been accustomed to suppose that the doctrine of divine predestination meant just this – that there already exists *now* a description of us and our future, including the choices we have not yet made, which is binding upon us, if only we knew it, because it is known to God. But I hope it is now clear that we should do God no honour by such a claim; for we should merely be inviting ourselves to imagine him in a logical self-contradiction. At this moment, we are unaware of any such description; so if it existed it would have to describe us as *not believing it*. But in that case we would be in error to believe it, for our believing it would falsify it! On the other hand, it would be of no use to alter the description so that it describes us as *believing it*; for in that case it is at the moment false, and therefore, although it would become correct if we believed it, we are not in error to *dis*believe it! Thus the divine 'foreknowledge' of our future, oddly enough, has no unconditional logical claim upon us, unknown to us.

This, I believe, demonstrates a fallacy underlying both the theological dispute between Arminianism and Calvinism, and the philosophical dispute between physical or psychological determinism (in the technical scientific sense) and libertarianism in relation to man's responsibility. What I am suggesting is that even God's sovereignty over every twist and turn of our drama does not contradict (*i.e.* offers no valid alternative to) our belief that we are free, in the sense that no determining specification already exists which if only we knew it we should be correct to believe and in error to disbelieve, whether we liked it or not.

In order to be clear that this is a logical point, rather than a theological one, let us notice how it applies also to the case of Hamlet and Shakespeare which we discussed in chapter 7. We, who know the whole drama from beginning to end, are in a position to make 'deterministic' statements about Hamlet's choices. We may say, for example, 'Hamlet decides to kill the king – Shakespeare has foreordained it.' But now let us ask ourselves, Is this a statement which Hamlet himself would have been correct to believe if only he had known it? Can we claim that, although Hamlet, poor fellow, supposed himself to be making a free choice, the truth is that he was bound to do what he did, and that he was merely ignorant of the truth in thinking otherwise? Of course not. Our description of Hamlet as deciding to kill the king, though valid from *our* viewpoint, would be not just false but logically *nonsensical* from Hamlet's until he had made up his mind. I am not referring now to the impossibility of Hamlet's getting to hear of the statement. What I am saying is that the statement, if brought before a court of logicians, would be judged to have no validity for Hamlet before the event; for its validity depends on Hamlet's *not* believing it. A Hamlet who believed such a statement would in effect have made up his mind and therefore would not, and could not, be in the same state as the Hamlet to whom the statement refers, who had not yet made up his mind.

For him, therefore, it is self-nullifying. Thus in Hamlet's (created) world, no complete description of his future exists or could exist, which would be equally correct whether he believed it or not: which would have an *unconditional claim to his assent* if only he knew it. In this sense his future is 'logically indeterminate', until he makes up his mind.

It may be objected that Hamlet's is only an imaginary world, whereas ours is real; but this, though true and important as a limitation of the analogy, does not affect the logical point, that what a creator knows about his creatures is *not* necessarily something that *they* would inevitably be correct to believe (and in error to disbelieve) if only they knew it. The point is that such a notion in particular cases is self-contradictory.

Criminal responsibility

If the foregoing argument is correct it would seem at one stroke to dispose of a great deal of the alleged conflict between psychology and religion. Take for example the vexed question of criminal responsibility. I referred in chapter 1 to the argument, 'It ain't my fault, judge, it's me glands.' For the typical healthy criminal, the answer suggested by what I have been saying is not 'It is your fault, it is not your glands', but 'It is your fault and (no doubt) it is your glands too'. Talk about your glands is talk about how the machinery runs. Talk about its being your fault is talk about the significance of the running of that machinery. It is a confusion of issues to discuss in unqualified terms whether we should treat all criminals as 'sick' or as 'guilty'. Viewed from the standpoint of society, any criminal may perhaps be classified as 'unhealthy' in his attitudes, and so in that sense 'sick'. But to conclude from this that we are entitled to insult the man by denying him responsibility for his actions would be totally unjustified and inhumane. If the foregoing argument is sound, this is something which can be done only if there is evidence that the 'sickness' in principle enables predictions of actions to be made (or at least implies the existence of predictions) which are equally binding upon the man whether he knows them or not, or likes them or not. In cases of brain damage or disease, for example, there may well be actions which *are* inevitable in this sense for the man concerned. To the extent that they are, we must recognize his responsibility to be diminished or even absent altogether. Note, however, that the distinction we need here is not one between actions which did, and did not, have mechanistic explanations, but rather between actions which were, and were not, inevitable-for-the-agent, even if *all* of them had mechanistic explanations.

This distinction has further implications in sociology where generalizations are typically made in terms of man in the mass. For example, out of a slum offering a certain environment it might be possible to predict that $x\%$ of children will become criminals. On the basis of this, it might be supposed that these criminals could be denied responsibility for their actions: that it was already 'fixed and inevitable' that they would develop as they did. But was it? Suppose that you and I were sociologists, and that on the basis of observations we could predict that a certain child will be in prison in a year's time. If we wanted that prediction to come true, we might have to take a plane to a desert island, or in some other way to ensure that our prediction (and we ourselves) could have no significant influence on the situation. We could then come back after a while to see whether the prediction was fulfilled. Assuming that it was, could we then honestly say, 'You see, it was already fixed and inevitable that this would happen'? Of course not. In the first place, our prediction would not necessarily have had any unconditional claim to the assent of the child himself, for the reasons we have already considered: it has been calculated on the assumption that he does *not* hear of or believe it. Secondly, the prediction did not even have an unconditional claim to *our* assent.

For at the time we made our prediction it would equally have been possible for us to take a different attitude. We could have said, 'This is terrible, what shall we do about it?' And by participating in the situation, doing our utmost to improve the conditions of the individual, and so forth, we would have completely upset the whole basis of our former prediction. Thus, so far from being 'fixed and inevitable', ours was merely a conditional description, which in effect faced us with a question: Do you want this to happen or not? The idea of physical or sociological determinism (in the technical scientific sense) as leading to an impersonal, mindless grind of inevitable events (moral determinism) is logically nonsense.

Let us be clear. What I am saying is not that in retrospect we can find no mechanistic explanation of what *has* happened; it is rather that, *until* the key choices have been made, no such story exists which is already binding upon the people who have to make the choices, if only they knew it; and that even after the event, no story can be found that they *would* have been unconditionally correct to believe and in error to disbelieve before the event, if only they had known it. Thus, in so far as sociologists are agents in their own story, it would be nonsense for a sociologist or his readers to imagine that *all* his possible predictions of 'choice behaviour' are inevitably fixed and binding upon him and everybody else as individuals, if only they knew it. However valid on the average, such mechanistic predictions in general have no power to prevent individuals as such from deciding, and ensuring, that this shall not apply to *them*.

The wholeness of human nature

Let me try to draw some threads together. What I have been suggesting in this and the previous chapter is that, in order to think clearly about the relation between scientific and biblical ideas of man, we need a particularly stringent mental discipline. We have constantly to keep in mind the difference between giving a complete explanation of the *mechanism* of a certain pattern of activity, and debunking its *significance* as personal agency. This will not, of course, prevent Christians from being asked why the biblical account of personal agency should be believed. An unbeliever has a right to expect to be shown how that account invites test in his own experience, on the one condition that he be willing to follow up the consequences of whatever he discovers to be true in it.[3]

But what I particularly want to emphasize is that there is no scriptural warrant for disputing the possibility of mechanistic description and explanation in an effort to safeguard the spiritual significance that the Bible attaches to us. Our nature has a multiplicity of complementary aspects, and no single account at one level of explanation can do full justice to all. In this sense man is indeed a mystery. Even to explain man's brain and body completely, if we could, in mechanistic terms, would not begin to dispose of the mystery which confronts us in the fact that, when all is said and done, here we are as cognitive agents who can contemplate the result. Where do *we* come into the mechanistic description? The answer I am suggesting is that we do not come into it – any more than the 'No smoking' message comes into the ink description, any more than the mathematical problem comes into the electronic engineer's description of the computing machine. These things are missed by mechanistic analysis. But they are not only equally matters of fact; they are the things that matter most.

What is most indubitable to each of us is that here we are, with a problem on our minds. This is the primary datum; this is the platform on which we build even our doubts; and this is precisely the kind of fact about us which the mechanistic analysis of our brain and body misses out, not because it is incompetent or scientifically incomplete, but because its categories are chosen for a different and complementary purpose.

In summary, then, if we would understand what the Bible has to say about our human nature we must try to appreciate the *wholeness* of the biblical concept of man, as a unity of body, mind and spirit. There is absolutely no basis for the idea that the biblical doctrine, in all its fullness, raises any kind of barrier to the mechanistic explanation of

[3] See chapter 10.

human activity. Since it follows that scientific discoveries in this area can provide no crucial test of Christian doctrine, it is only realistic and fair, when Christians talk to non-Christians, to point out that evidence of the truth of Christianity must be sought elsewhere; and here the converse point applies. No conceivable result of brain research can offer any excuse for not investigating the Bible's own offered grounds of conviction, both historical and experiential, that what it reveals is the true point and purpose of our existence.

Postscript

The argument from 'logical indeterminacy' is discussed in more detail, and some of the objections to it answered, in:

MacKay, D. M., 'The Sovereignty of God in the Natural World', *Scottish Journal of Theology*, 21 (1968), pp. 13-36.

MacKay, D. M., *Freedom of Action in a Mechanistic Universe* (Eddington Lecture), (Cambridge University Press, 1967). Reprinted in *Good Readings in Psychology*, edited by M. S. Gazzaniga and E. P. Lovejoy (Prentice Hall, 1971), pp. 121-138.

MacKay, D. M., 'Choice in a Mechanistic Universe', *British Journal of the Philosophy of Science*, 22 (1971), pp. 275-285.

MacKay, D. M., 'The Logical Indeterminateness of Human Choices', *British Journal of the Philosophy of Science*, 24 (1973), pp. 405-408.

9. Educating for freedom

The theme of this book has been the essential, non-accidental, harmony between biblical Christian faith and mechanistic science. The scientific approach, as we have seen, is not just uneasily compatible with biblical theism, but rather positively encouraged by it. The events of our physical world are, from the Christian standpoint, the continual gifts of a faithful and non-capricious Creator. In those events we discern a mechanistic pattern on which we have learnt (and are encouraged by biblical doctrine) to rely in all normal circumstances as a guide to our plans and expectations. The mechanistic thought-models of modern science thus spell out in one particular form the very same trust in the faithfulness of God that the Bible inculcates more generally in the man of faith. In this sense science and faith are one. Any separation between them is artificial; for the one is meant to be but an outworking of the other in one and the same spirit of humble dependence and readiness to obey the truth.

The freedom and autonomy of science, then, on which we have laid so much emphasis as a thoroughly biblical notion, is only *methodological* and not *ontological*.[1] Science, in other words, is not an alternative to God as the source of truth, but a specialized way of gathering and discovering patterns in data which Christians believe to have one and the same Source. The discipline of science is autonomous in the sense that we need not have explicit theological convictions in order to practise it. It has developed and been

[1] 'Ontological autonomy' would mean that science set itself up as an independent source of truth *alongside* God.

88

moulded under pressure of the data themselves – data to whose implications Christian and non-Christian alike find they must be obedient if their scientific enterprise is to succeed. Christians believe that these implications are God-ordained; but biblical revelation provides no basis for inferring *a priori* what they are in detail. All it offers is a rational incentive to look for them in the proper way in the data of the natural world.

It follows from all this that the bogey of machine-mindedness can be exorcized without grubbing around for phenomena that have no mechanistic explanation. There may well be such phenomena; certainly mechanistic science has no way of proving that there are not. But the chief mis-understanding that underlies machine-mindedness is only reinforced if its opponents concentrate on these things; for the most important limits of mechanistic explanation are not territorial but conceptual. Moreover, as we have seen, they are *self-imposed* for a deliberately and necessarily limited purpose.

To explain in mechanistic terms is to move to a stand-point from which other aspects of the situation may become invisible or irrelevant – but it is not in the least to devalue those aspects in their own context. Whether it be true or false that all natural happenings have a mechanistic ex-planation, the notion says nothing – absolutely nothing – either for or against their continual dependence on God in the sense implied by biblical theism. That more funda-mental aspect, vitally meaningful for the Christian as he wrestles with the real world of daily life, is strictly and properly excluded from the game of mechanistic explana-tion.

Again, whether or not the workings of our brains are fully mechanistic, we have seen that the possibility that they are offers no threat to (or escape from) the solemn reality of our responsibility as human beings. If we are concerned to defend the spiritual nature and dignity of man, there is no need to hunt for processes in the brain that defy mechanistic explanation. There may be many such, for all we know; but woe betide us if we suggest that human dignity is the kind of thing that depends on keeping them inexplicable when viewed at the physical level.

How then can people best be educated to see the fallacy in machine-mindedness, and to develop a healthy and fearless respect both for science and for the religious values that nourished its growth? The need is urgent. For many would-be humane writers today, unfortunately, 'educating for freedom' seems to be a matter of reactionary doublethink: of turning our backs on what the pestiferous scientists are doing, and hoping that at least in our lifetime they will not discover enough to make it awkward for us. If we dismiss this response as tragically misguided and inadequate, it seems reasonable to ask what positive alternative suggests itself from a Christian standpoint. How can we help people to get the virus out of their system?

Half the battle will be won, I believe, by what those of us who teach, write or preach on science do *not* say. It is by the philosophical and theological blunders we do not commit, by the anti-scientific fear or the scientistic arrogance we do not express, and by the weak arguments on which we do not teach them to rely, that we may do most good.

But of course we are confronted with a disease that has already taken root, and positive remedies are needed too. First among these from a logical standpoint is to expose the fallacy of 'nothing-buttery'. This we looked at in chapter 4. The idea that one and the same situation may need two or more accounts, each *complete* at its own logical level, may sound abstract and difficult. But as we have seen, it can be illustrated by innumerable familiar examples, and it simply must be grasped if people are to think rationally about the implications of science. Different levels of description of reality are logically necessary in order to express all that truthfully needs to be said about it. When properly disciplined, these are not rivals, but complementary, in the sense that each reveals an aspect which is there to be reckoned with, but is unmentioned in the other.

Complementarity

In speaking of 'complementarity' here one has to guard against several misunderstandings. Readers who are familiar with the 'complementarity' of the wave and particle pictures of matter or light are liable to think of it as a physical rather than a logical notion, and to suspect an argument by analogy from physics. Again, the fact that an architect's plan and elevation drawings offer a simple geometrical example of complementarity may give the impression that all complementary descriptions are logically the same in kind. But in all the cases we have been considering the different levels of description form a kind of hierarchy: one level is 'higher' than the other, in the sense that it presupposes the other, and reveals its significance in fresh categories. Thus, to hark back to the example of the signboard which we used in chapter 3, the description of the situation as an advertisement presupposes, and reveals the significance of, its description as a mass of flashing lamps. The two descriptions are 'hierarchically complementary'. If there is any advertisement on the board, there must be an electrically-explicable pattern of lamp-flashes; but not every conceivable pattern of lamp-flashes spells an advertisement.

So when we speak of scientific and religious categories or descriptions as complementary, there is no suggestion that the two are conceptually on the same level, like the north and east views of a mountain, or the front and side views of a building. These illustrations help to make the point that different descriptions of the same situation do not necessarily conflict; but they cannot be pressed as a detailed analogy. What must be emphasized is that the religious account of reality is logically 'higher' than the scientific: it presupposes that some scientific description can be given of the world of created events, and goes beyond it by claiming to reveal the significance of those events. In this sense, as we have noted already, the biblical-theistic account of reality embraces the scientific.

'Doublethink'

Finally in this connection, it needs to be made clear that the idea of 'complementarity' offers no licence for undisciplined 'doublethink', for dishonestly having it both ways where the truth admits of only one way. There are perhaps too few safeguards against this in the contemporary 'theology of paradox'. It is surely crucial, if we claim to serve the God of truth, to encourage people to think critically, and to chew with sharp logical teeth on any claim that two superficially disparate statements are complementary. As we saw in chapter 4, there are logical tests to distinguish genuinely complementary from contradictory statements. Complementarity is not an arbitrary notion to be invoked or rejected as a matter of whim or argumentative strategy. Whether two statements are logically complementary is a question of fact, on which we can be right or wrong.

For the same reason, however, those of us who abhor the woolliness of paradox-mongering must beware of oversimplifying issues that involve genuinely complementary categories, creating artificial conflicts under the impression that it is always more honest to make black-and-white contradictions out of disparate descriptions. We would all agree that there is no merit, for example, in creating a spurious opposition between an electrical and a mathematical explanation of the workings of a computer! The unbridled lust for simple 'either/ors' needs to be resisted just as strongly as any sneaking desire to 'have it both ways'; for it can be fruitful of just as serious distortions of truth. 'Either God or chance'; 'either the work of the Holy Spirit or the working of psychological machinery'; 'either divine creation or biological evolution': all these have a brave sound of 'no compromise' about them; but in nine cases out of ten they represent a pathetic sell-out of truth to the nothing-buttery of the opposition.[2] It is only where we can demonstrate that the truth of a theistic claim would logically rule out the truth of a scientific one, or *vice versa*, that we have a right and duty to see them as opposites.

[2] See Chapter 5.

Personal versus mechanical?

One of the commonest misconceptions of what I have been expounding is that where two or more descriptions are complementary, both are equally good and one can opt for one or the other according to taste. Why then bother to use personal categories at all for human behaviour? Behind this notion there is often a presupposition picked up from second-rate books of popular science that the ideal way to understand any situation is to start with the atoms and build up. And if we start from atoms, where on earth does consciousness come in?

Of course, as we saw in chapters 4 and 8, along that road consciousness does not come in. Why should it? The notion, popularized by writers like Teilhard de Chardin, that if men are conscious there must be some traces of consciousness in atoms, is quite without rational foundation. Logically it makes no more sense than arguing that if I write an English sentence in chalk, there must be something English about each of the chalk particles! Consciousness is not something we expect to be forced to recognize as the end-product of an argument about the behaviour of physical particles, like magnetic force, or interstellar gas. The reality of the situation is that we *start* as conscious beings. We should not have any questions if we were not. It is to the data of our conscious experience that all our thinking, and even our doubting, must do justice; for these are data that we would be lying to deny.

Starting on solid ground

So if we want to start with our feet on solid ground, here it is. The prevalent notion that the firmest starting-point of thought is the world of atoms is philosophically bankrupt and must be resisted; it turns the reality of the situation upside down. Once seen in realistic perspective, the problem becomes not to discover where consciousness comes into the atomic story, but rather to discover what atomic (or other mechanistic) story (if any) correlates with the conscious

93

experience to which we can and must truthfully bear witness. This is an open-ended technical question of psychophysiology, with no tendentious implications whatsoever. If people can once be helped to recognize and correct the popular inversion of priorities at this point, they will be proof against much of the superficial plausibility of machine-mindedness.

Freedom versus unpredictability

In addition to all these points, it is vital to help people to distinguish freedom, in the sense necessary for responsibility, from mere *unpredictability*. So often freedom is thought of as something like the unpredictable behaviour shown by a coin when tossed. No doubt there is a certain kind of human spontaneity or caprice which is exciting in much the same way: 'Who could have guessed he would do that?' But I suggest that this 'freedom' of caprice, unpredictable by anyone, is quite a different notion from the freedom necessary for moral action. For the reasons sketched in chapter 8, I think it would be a complete betrayal of the concept of *moral* freedom to insist on unpredictability-by-anyone as a necessary condition, and to deny a man responsibility for an action just because it was or could have been predicted by a detached observer. As we saw earlier, *predictability by non-participants* is not the same as *inevitability for the agent*. This may be a more difficult point than most, because it cuts across our instinctive presupposition that what is correctly believed by a detached observer is always by definition what everyone would be correct to believe if only they knew it. As we saw in chapter 8, in relation to beliefs about ourselves this presupposition is clearly false. Much effort will be needed to repair the damage it has done to our thinking about human freedom and responsibility.

A unified perspective

But behind all these particular issues – some relatively straightforward, others admittedly complex – lies the greatest educational need of our time, to restore *wholeness* to our view of life. The machine-image promises unification of a kind – but only at the cost of leaving out, as irrational and fragmentary oddities, those human questions and concerns and values about which we feel most deeply. What is the point of it all?

I have made no secret of my conviction that the only complete solvent of machine-mindedness, and the only perfect education for freedom, is in a proper conception of God as author of our whole lives, including the marvellously intricate mechanistic story that our science is uncovering.

It is such a pathetic betrayal of truth to allow to grow in people's minds the idea that 'God had it all his own way until science came along and discovered mechanistic explanation'. To spread the idea deliberately, as some atheists do, seems sheer dishonesty when one thinks that from the biblical-theistic standpoint it is to God's own creative faithfulness, the faithfulness and regularity of his sustaining in being the universe that he has created, that we owe the success and worthwhileness of our mechanistic enterprise in science. It is *his* story that we are trying to tell in our mechanistic terms. This conviction was one of the major motive factors in the rise of modern science; and it is not without significance that the great majority of the most famous developers of the mechanistic world model – Newton, Boyle, Faraday, Maxwell, Compton, Eddington come to mind as examples – were believers in God. Their belief gave them all the greater confidence in the worthwhileness of studying nature. It is in the biblical doctrine of God as the Creator of our whole drama, its mechanistic level as well as its personal, that I see the one unifying perspective for the scientifically-structured world in which we live.

This doctrine of course does not stand alone. I believe that if we are to help people towards a unified perspective, the wholeness of the doctrine of God as we find it in the Bible is necessary. Experience has shown that the more theologians try to make it palatable to modern man by whittling it away, the deeper they find themselves in inconsistencies of their own making.

In particular, if our freedom is to be adult and mature, I believe we need the whole doctrine of the sovereignty of God. As we saw in the previous chapter, the predestinarian story of our world as seen by its Author no more denies our freedom as agents in it than does the mechanistic story about our brains. It is a fallacy in logic to suggest that we must soft-pedal divine sovereignty in order to get by with a view of man as truly free and dignified. Quite on the contrary, I believe that our true dignity is rooted in the biblical doctrine of the sovereignty of God, which leaves us even more clearly responsible before him than if we had never heard of it.

A Christian understanding of freedom is rooted in the idea that God has had a purpose in mind for each of us; that we are not just the spawn of a biological process for which he touched a button long ago, but we are also the characters in a drama, each individual one of whom has been thought into being for a personal purpose and indeed for his glory within that drama. Here, for me, there is the only possible coherent answer to the question we must now face in our concluding chapter: freedom – for what?

10. Freedom – for what?

One of the lessons learnt early in nursery life, and amply driven home later, is that freedom without a worthy object becomes a curse. Perhaps to men under totalitarian constraint this would seem an academic point; but in more favoured societies in our day there is plenty of evidence that aimless freedom is not enough. It is a commonplace – though not less true for that – that where men cease to believe in God they have to make a god of something less.

What need for God?

It should be clear from what has been said already that mechanistic science, understood for what it is, gives no support to the dismissal of God. It leaves as much room for belief in God as ever biblical theism required, and indeed finds fundamental support in that belief. But this alone, of course, offers no positive reason to believe in God. Indeed, I think that Christians ought to insist that there is no need for the idea of 'God' in the field of ordinary scientific explanation. If Laplace ever actually made the often-quoted remark 'I have no need of that hypothesis' (when asked why he had not brought 'God' into his equations) I think he was right. He was right, because to bring God in there would be as absurd as if we, watching the artist's cricket match we discussed in chapter 6, were to try to find a need to invoke the artist to explain what the players were doing. In the created world, we have no need of 'the artist' for that kind of explanation.

But of course what the Bible urges upon us is not that we

will find it necessary intellectually to keep referring to the idea of God, or to bring God in as part of every explanation of events. The point it makes is rather that, whether or not we find it intellectually necessary, it happens to be true that our world is, in sober fact, God's created world, with all that this implies. We shall always find ourselves at cross purposes with the Bible unless we realize that it is not out to provide satisfying answers to speculative questions. It is essentially a practical testimony; and its aim is not to satisfy speculative enquiries, but to make us face relevant facts.

What, then, are the facts whose relevance requires us to reckon with God? First, there is the fact of our dependence on the creative will of God. This, as we noted, would have no relevance at all in daily life were it not that God has chosen a particular kind of active relationship with the world he has created.[1] I want to stress this, because people sometimes suppose that it should be possible to argue logically to belief in God purely from consideration of the natural world. Even if someone accepts the doctrine of the dependence of our world on God, in its theistic sense, I should still say that if the Bible had stopped there he might reasonably answer, 'So what?' But the Bible of course goes on. Its theme is that the whole point and purpose of our existence and our dependence on God, the whole reason why God has thought such a world into being, with each of us in it, is that we should be invited into a personal relationship with him which it calls *love*, in a deeper and stronger sense than we often allow that poor word to bear. A relationship of love with our own Creator: that is the purpose of our life, the end for which we have been brought into being. Rightly or wrongly, that is what the Bible tells us. That is why its claim is important, whatever we may do about it; because if it is true, then nothing matters more.

But further, and a little deeper under the skin, it goes on to point out something to which the consciences of most of us assent, if we let it sink in: that in our natural state we are not worthy of this relationship with a God of perfect

[1] See chapter 6.

love and perfect justice. Worse than that, we are not even pining for it. This unworthiness, this reluctance, indeed hopelessness *vis-à-vis* God, is what we noted earlier as the essence of our sin, or sinfulness.[2] This shows itself in all kinds of individual sins. But they are only the symptoms, the 'spots on the face' as it were; what matters is the underlying disease. The root of the trouble is our basic unreadiness to allow God the run of our lives; and this the Bible urges us to recognize as a fault that needs forgiveness and remedy beyond our own unaided strength.

The need for rescue

Here, then, we have the biblical answer to the question: 'What is the need for God?' Notice that this is not now the intellectual need for the *idea* of God: it is a real need for *God*, for God's power, for God to do something about us. For if it is true that God has brought us into being for a relationship of deep, strong love, and obedience, and eager happiness with him; and if by nature we are disinclined for this; and if we have no power ourselves to change that disinclination radically; then, if God is himself willing to change us and give us this love for him, we need him. We need him more than we need anything else in the world; for as long as we resist or ignore him we are missing the main point and purpose of our very existence.

This relationship is not, of course, in a vacuum. We do not have to withdraw from the world in order to enter into it. The point is rather that we live through every day's ordinary events either with him, in love with him, in his service, and to his glory, or else with our backs to him, our opportunities wasted and ruined in what amounts to rebellion. These, according to the Bible, are the options that face each of us every day. That is why it is so important to ask ourselves: Is this true? And if it is true, how can we know it?

This is not the place to give a detailed answer to these questions. The point I want to make is that they are dealt with fully, in practical terms, in the Bible itself. The New

[2] See chapter 8.

Testament in particular spells out the way in which God is able and ready to deal with what needs to be set right in us, and between us and him. It points out that our discomfort at the thought of God is a reflection of our long history, both as a race and as individuals, of offences against his love and justice, the way we have rejected him in self-will through our lives. It points out, too, that this needs *atonement*: we need to be rescued or 'redeemed' from the power of evil in order to be free. It goes on to give the message which earned the gospel from the first the name of 'good news': that what Jesus Christ did in accepting death was to suffer *for us* the consequences of this, our rejection of God; and that in his own sufferings, in a deep and mysterious sense, he atoned for our sinfulness on behalf of all who are prepared on God's terms to accept that atonement as a free gift, living henceforth in the new relationship of loving obedience and dependence on his strength for which we were created.

All this may be familiar doctrine to many of us; but let us not miss the force of it in the present context. For this is the only rational answer to the man who asks why he needs biblical categories in addition to scientific ones. If it is true, then clearly nothing that a man will meet in the whole of his life can be more important. Although it may well lose its impact by repetition, I think there is for each of us a first time at which he hears it realistically, as something addressed to him, personally. Even though he has heard it all his life until then, he comes to understand for the first time why it is called 'good news': for he finds that to work out what it means personally, and to close with it, accepting on God's terms the new kind of life that he is longing to make possible, leads into that purposeful freedom that the New Testament calls 'life eternal', life more abundant: life which is really worth living.

The test of experience

How then can an honest man, in this age, become convinced that all this is true, in such a way that he would be aware of dishonesty, of untruth, if he were to turn his back

100

on it? Jesus faced a question like that more than once. On one notable occasion when a great discussion was going on among the Jews about his credentials and authority Jesus replied: 'Whoever has the will to do the will of God shall know whether my teaching comes from him or is merely my own.'[3] Here, I suggest, we have basically an appeal to all that is true and honest in the *scientific* attitude: an appeal to test for yourself, to allow your own experience an opportunity to bear out the truth of what he claims. Of course the whole context of the Bible, and indeed the experience of other Christians who have lived out its teaching, may be necessary to guide us in discovering how to set about making this test. And it will be no isolated experience, but an ongoing process of daily interaction with God for the rest of our lives that will attest the authority that Christ has claimed. But what I am stressing is that we are not asked to accept this solely as an intellectual belief, on someone else's authority, without any consequences that will attest its reality. Not 'knowing *about* God', but '*knowing* God', is what the Bible refers to as 'eternal life'.[4]

If Christ speaks truly, then his doctrine has, indeed, the authority of God; but for us to *know* that it has God's authority, it is not necessary for us to mortgage our intellect, or indulge in wishful thinking. Christ's own suggestion is that the scientific spirit of eager openness and readiness to put ourselves in the way of evidence, coupled with faithful and humble obedience to what we know and discover, can lead the way to growing conviction. As we noted in chapter 3, there are important contrasts between this approach and the search for scientific knowledge-in-detachment. The test that Christ invites is one that we cannot make unless we are prepared to be involved up to our necks – a test that will exercise every faculty we have and challenge the autonomy of our will in the process. So the approach in a scientific spirit does not mean saying, 'All right; I'll make the experiment if I can keep myself detached.' That would

[3] John 7 : 17 (NEB).
[4] John 17 : 3. For a helpful analysis see J. I. Packer, *Knowing God* (Hodder, 1973).

simply amount to saying, 'I won't make the experiment.' Scientific 'openness to evidence' here demands that if we want evidence of the truth, we must be prepared to satisfy the conditions upon which evidence is promised.

It is important not to confuse this readiness for evidence with 'begging the question' or 'believing in order to see what happens'. According to Christ, when a man gets down to face realistically the question 'If God keeps his promise to show you that this is his will, will you do it?', he is already taking the first step towards knowing the reality of God himself. If he works out in detail what Christ's teaching would mean for him, he will soon enough discover the truth of Christ's diagnosis of his own condition. If at each step he responds honestly and realistically, Christ's promise is that he will find himself indeed at grips with a living Reality, whose claims he has to reckon with whether he likes it or not. In this context I find that the scientific spirit, so far from being an embarrassment, is if anything a help. For if there is one emphasis that a scientist is ideally trained to respect, it is the emphasis on realism in facing facts. 'If this is true, let's face it.' There could be no better spirit in which to approach the Christian gospel.

Freedom with a purpose

As the conviction dawns and grows that Christ has spoken the sober truth about us and the purpose of our existence, and that his priorities are the right ones for us, we can expect our concept of freedom itself to be illuminated and changed. The freedom we will want above all is freedom to meet and live up to the claims that our Creator has upon us: claims as of right, the claims of creatorship.

Note that in all this we will need God's initiative not just to co-operate with us, as if we had all the right ideas and just needed to bring him in to help us carry them through, but rather to liberate us from our warped perspective on what is best. We will need him to rescue us again and again from the self-centredness that sometimes makes us prefer not to know what he knows to be best, because we should like to have a bit of initiative of our own. This self-destructive rebellion, which so often masquerades under the banner of 'freedom', is perhaps the most subtle manifestation of our fallenness. It is the besetting weakness of our humanity to mistake licence for liberty.

By the same token, it is a source of strength and joy for the Christian to have his eyes progressively opened to his true priorities, spurred by a sense of infinitely deep obligation to the One who has rescued him. The glad working out of this obligation day by day, in the light of what God has revealed of his will, is the practical answer of the Bible to the question: 'Freedom for what?' We have an irreducible responsibility, both to him and, as he has taught us, to our fellow men no less. This two-sided responsibility is what sets the target for our freedom. In meeting it we find our deepest happiness and fulfilment.

11. Retrospect

The good name of science is at risk. It has been prostituted in the interests of many causes. In this book I have tried, as fairly as I could, to set the record straight in areas where science has been grossly abused or misunderstood to the detriment of morality and religion. Our conclusion has been that the nourishment of science by biblical faith in its early days was no accident of history, but reflects permanent features of the nature of each. We have rejected as over-simple the image of the two as independent, parallel sources of truth. Their relationship is more intimate than that. We could better say that science, as a humble and eager and scrupulously careful response to the data of the natural world, is one expression of that obedience to the Creator which biblical faith inculcates in all departments of life. In this sense biblical faith not merely tolerates but embraces the scientific approach, while encouraging the *methodological* autonomy that is proper for its purpose.

To leave the matter there, however, would have been misleading in its turn. For if the God of Christian faith were no more than a distant Creator, his existence would be of little more than academic interest. What makes Christianity urgently relevant to real life is the other side of the biblical-theistic picture, which shows God as our Rescuer from the futile rebelliousness of self-centred living, as the One whose love for us is stronger than death, and who waits to implant in us a corresponding love for himself in return. In this context also, biblical theism encourages an approach in the authentic spirit of science, asking: If this be true, what then? Is it true? How is an honest man supposed to discover it to be so?

To answer this question at all adequately we have had to look at some of the detailed implications of the Christian gospel. I make no apology for this, however. For it is in the biblical picture as an integrated whole, as something whose elements hang together and make sense together, that I believe we have a unifying perspective from which the advance of science can be welcomed without fear of determinism, depersonalization or demoralization. It answers our question 'Freedom – for what?' not with a formula but in terms of an ongoing relationship – a day-by-day working out of the purpose of our creation with our Creator, whom to worship is to obey. If we ask why, historically, this biblical Christian perspective has been ousted in so many quarters, we will see from the literature that time and again it has been through a false, logically mistaken set of would-be conclusions from mechanistic science. Misconceptions of the relation of scientific explanation to theistic doctrine have been made responsible for the dismissal of key doctrines which may well have been unpalatable for other reasons also. One of the greatest tragedies of our age is that so many Christians allowed themselves, particularly in the last century, to be frightened away from proclaiming the full message of biblical Christianity by the notion that it was scientifically out of date or discredited. The greatest possible service that Christians can render to the cause of true freedom, I believe, will be to help recover for our generation the old but ever new and true faith of which we have thus wrongly and mistakenly been robbed in the name of science. They must seek to inculcate the truest realism, that reckons first with the fact of God and his purpose in creating us and his resources offered freely to all who are sincere with him and are ready for the consequences. They must seek to encourage us to the truest maturity, that is not above asking to be forgiven and to be remade into the image that our self-centredness and self-will has defaced. It is not for nothing that the saints of the ages have testified that in his service alone there is perfect freedom.

Appendix

Some common misunderstandings of the argument from 'logical indeterminacy'

I am indebted to a number of correspondents and critics who have expressed the following misunderstandings of points raised in the argument of chapters 7 and 8 on the nature of man. Readers who find themselves in difficulty might care to use them as check-points. In each case, what the argument has been *thought* to say is presented first in quotation marks, and followed by my comments.

1. 'You are saying that the mind is only one facet of the brain's activity.' – No. What I argue is that mental activity and brain activity are each *complementary* aspects of the greater unity that is our human activity.

2. 'By calling these complementary, you imply that the mental and the physical aspects are on much the same level, as for example the wave- and the particle-aspects of the nature of light.' – Not at all. The complementary levels of explanation here form a hierarchy. It is as conscious beings that we learn anything about the physical world; so there is a sense in which the reality of our conscious experience has priority over anything we believe about our brains or anything else. To rest content with the brain-story would be to miss the main point of what it is to be a human being.

3. 'So you think that free will can be accounted for in purely physical terms?' – No. It is only the brain *activity* that mediates free choice which I have allowed (for the sake of argument) to be so accounted for.

4. 'But you are putting forward a view of man as a

purely physical being.' – No. See (2) above. I am allowing (for the sake of argument) the possibility that all the individual elements of man's brain-and-body may interact according to purely physical laws. Explanation at this level, however, would leave unmentioned and hence unexplained a whole hierarchy of questions framed in personal and other higher-level categories. We must not confuse the ability of science to *account for all events* in its own terms with the ability to *answer all questions*. This confusion underlies the fallacy of metaphysical reductionism or 'nothing-buttery'.

5. 'You concede determinism to the opposition.' – I do not 'concede' any kind of determinism in the sense of agreeing with it. I simply ask what *would* follow if (*physical*) determinism were granted. I claim to show that even if it were granted, *metaphysical* determinism (denying the reality of human freedom and responsibility) would not follow logically from it. I therefore urge Christians and others interested in maintaining respect for human dignity and responsibility not to waste their ammunition on *physical* determinism, even of the 'softer' variety which has come in with the Heisenberg uncertainty principle.

7. 'Your argument makes people's freedom depend on whether someone tries to tell them what they are going to do.' – This confuses moral freedom with unpredictability-by-others (see 13 below). For a man to be morally free, there must not exist a complete prediction of his action that (if only he knew it) he would be correct to accept as inevitable whether he liked it or not. Put positively, he must have the power to falsify, if he wanted to, any proffered prediction of his behaviour, even when that prediction would have been fulfilled if he had not known of it. As pointed out in chapter 8, man's freedom in this sense could in principle be established without actually offering him any prediction; and his action need not be unpredictable by observers.

8. 'By this criterion, a man may be right to feel "free" before the event; but afterwards he could be shown that he really was not free.' – He could certainly in principle be shown afterwards that his choice was not *unpredictable-by-*

observers. This would not show that *he* was in error at the time in believing himself free. On the contrary, the same evidence would show that until he made up his mind, the outcome was up to him, and was logically indeterminate. For example, you could predict that a Scot like myself would always choose porridge in preference to cereals for breakfast. So I might; but I am still free to do otherwise, and could defy you to tell me with certainty that I shall choose porridge. My regularly choosing porridge is no less a free choice for being predictable.

9. 'The argument hangs on an arbitrary definition of "truth".' – The argument can be framed without using the word 'truth' at all. It is concerned with the conditions under which particular future-tense descriptions of human agents become self-invalidating for particular individuals. I do, as a matter of fact, prefer to reserve the word 'true' for propositions that anyone and everyone would be correct to believe and in error to disbelieve; but I do not think that this is particularly idiosyncratic; and in any case it is not a necessary assumption of my argument. What I do assume is that if someone claims that certain evidence about a man's brain refutes the man's belief that he is free, it must be shown that the man concerned would believe correctly if he were to believe the evidence in question. This does *not* imply that the man must be shown the evidence. But if A claims that evidence X refutes B's belief Y, this must imply that if only B knew X, B would be rationally obliged to give up Y.

10. 'The notion of freedom offered is purely subjective.' – Not at all. The question whether a prediction exists (unknown to the agent) with a well-founded unconditional claim to his assent is an objective question which could in principle be settled publicly behind the agent's back.

11. 'Would not the agent's believing his *own* subjective story make it out of date in just the same way as his believing an observer's description of his brain would make that out of date?' – This misses an important distinction between the relation of the agent to (a) his personal account of his experience and (b) the observer's story about his brain.

The brain-story has to establish its claim to A's assent by adducing supporting evidence. The agent's personal story, on the other hand, is not one that he has received with supporting evidence, but one that he has generated in an effort to bear witness truthfully to the data of his experience. His reason for telling it is not that he has been told it and has been convinced by evidence added to it, but rather that to deny it (on his part) would be to lie.

Thus whereas A's belief (or disbelief) in the brain-story depends on his giving (or withholding) *assent*, where his own personal story is concerned the agent does not have to go through any process of 'giving assent'; his relation to it is that of a truthful (or else a lying) *generator*. If you ask him 'Is it true that you have toothache?' you are not asking whether the proposition 'A has toothache' has an unconditional claim to A's assent, but rather whether A's experience has an unconditional claim to be expressed by A's saying 'I have toothache'.

12. 'If I decided to fulfil a prediction offered to me, the outcome would no longer be "logically indeterminate".' – This is a serious misunderstanding. The question is not whether you would be correct to believe that you will fulfil the prediction, but whether the prediction has an unconditional claim to your assent. If I have already decided to have another cup of tea, and feel sufficiently thirsty, I may well agree with you if you predict that I will have it. But this alone does not suffice to show that it is inevitable that I will have it, nor that there exists now a determinate specification of my future action with an unconditional claim to my assent. In order to establish such a claim, we would have to apply the variational test which is implied in the phrase 'whether you know it or not or like it or not'. In this respect the concept of inevitability is rather like the concept of stability in physics. When we describe a ball at the bottom of a bowl as 'stable', we mean more than that it is at rest; and we have to explicate what we mean by talking of what would happen if small perturbations of particular sorts took place. A similar point, I think, applies to the concept of 'freedom' itself. It needs to be spelt out by

saying what would, or would not, be the case in such and such circumstances.

13. 'You do not seem to recognize that other theories of freedom also have room for the concept of diminished responsibility.' – My suggestion is in fact the converse – that other 'libertarian' theories are too ready to *deny* responsibility in cases where it is thought that a complete mechanistic explanation of bodily behaviour could be given. I wish to argue that certain grounds on which other theories deny a man responsibility are invalid grounds.

14. 'Is this not a new concept of "freedom"?' – What I wish to point out is that by calling a man 'free' we might mean one of two quite different things: (a) We might mean that his action was *unpredictable by anyone*. This I would call the freedom of caprice; *or* (b) we may mean that the outcome of his decision is *up to him*, in the sense that unless he makes the decision it will not be made, that he is in a position to make it, and that no fully-determinate specification of the outcome already exists, which he would be correct to accept as inevitable, and would be unable to falsify, if only he knew it.

15. 'Does your theory not contradict the Bible's teaching that God always knows how people will respond to his communications to them?' – Nothing in what I have said denies that God-our-Creator knows, and is sovereign over, every detail of our past, present and future. What I do argue is that this divine foreknowledge is not something that *we* could be correct to believe if only we knew it – since for us (unlike God) this would involve a self-contradiction (see chapter 8).

16. 'But did not Christ know that he must fulfil what the prophets had written of him?' – The biblical evidence suggests that Christ indeed recognized what the prophets described was the will of his Father for him; and that he freely chose to fulfil that will. But this did not mean that the outcome was independent of his faithfulness to this decision, nor that he would have been correct to regard the outcome as already fixed and inevitable (witness his prayer, 'If it be possible, let this cup pass from me'). To choose to

fulfill a prediction is not the same as to make that prediction logically determinate and inevitable for the chooser.

17. 'Could not your whole argument be applied to a robot, which would then also have free will?' – The argument applies explicitly and only to cognitive agents, *i.e.* conscious beings who entertain beliefs, correctly or otherwise. The argument could not be applied to a robot unless by 'robot' was meant a *cognitive* agent artificially constructed. I know of no biblical reason for asserting that no artificially-constructed individual could be conscious; all I would say is that the man who claims that a robot is conscious has the onus of proof. It is not enough that the robot should have behaviour which *we* could interpret in personal terms; the question is whether there is anyone there before us, conscious of us, and capable of *believing* correctly or incorrectly, as distinct from a mere object capable of typing out the symbols in which *we* express beliefs. The essential point to bear in mind is that neither brains nor calculating machines as such 'have experience'; it is *persons* – conscious personal agents – and not their brains, of whom it makes sense to say that they have experience. The science-fiction question whether it might be possible one day to procreate (not 'create'!) human persons artificially cannot be settled dogmatically; but I do not think that the artificiality or otherwise of the procreation would or should be a decisive factor in determining the status of the choices made by such an individual, if he ever came into existence.

Index